Clarence Darrow's Last Trial

by Shirley Lauro

A Samuel French Acting Edition

New York Hollywood London Toronto

SAMUELFRENCH.COM

Copyright © 1985, 1992, 1996, 2009 by Shirley Lauro

ALL RIGHTS RESERVED

Cover image © New Theatre, Inc.
Actor pictured on cover: John Felix

CAUTION: Professionals and amateurs are hereby warned that *CLARENCE DARROW'S LAST TRIAL* is subject to a Licensing Fee. It is fully protected under the copyright laws of the United States of America, the British Commonwealth, including Canada, and all other countries of the Copyright Union. All rights, including professional, amateur, motion picture, recitation, lecturing, public reading, radio broadcasting, television and the rights of translation into foreign languages are strictly reserved. In its present form the play is dedicated to the reading public only.

The amateur live stage performance rights to *CLARENCE DARROW'S LAST TRIAL* are controlled exclusively by Samuel French, Inc., and licensing arrangements and performance licenses must be secured well in advance of presentation. PLEASE NOTE that amateur Licensing Fees are set upon application in accordance with your producing circumstances. When applying for a licensing quotation and a performance license please give us the number of performances intended, dates of production, your seating capacity and admission fee. Licensing Fees are payable one week before the opening performance of the play to Samuel French, Inc., at 45 W. 25th Street, New York, NY 10010.

Licensing Fee of the required amount must be paid whether the play is presented for charity or gain and whether or not admission is charged.

Stock licensing fees quoted upon application to Samuel French, Inc.

For all other rights than those stipulated above, apply to: Abrams Artists Agency, 275 Seventh Avenue, 26th Floor, New York, NY 10001, Att: Peter Hagan.

Particular emphasis is laid on the question of amateur or professional readings, permission and terms for which must be secured in writing from Samuel French, Inc.

Copying from this book in whole or in part is strictly forbidden by law, and the right of performance is not transferable.

Whenever the play is produced the following notice must appear on all programs, printing and advertising for the play: "Produced by special arrangement with Samuel French, Inc."

Due authorship credit must be given on all programs, printing and advertising for the play.

ISBN 978-0-573-69706-7   Printed in U.S.A.   #29307

> No one shall commit or authorize any act or omission by which the copyright of, or the right to copyright, this play may be impaired.

> No one shall make any changes in this play for the purpose of production.

> Publication of this play does not imply availability for performance. Both amateurs and professionals considering a production are strongly advised in their own interests to apply to Samuel French, Inc., for written permission before starting rehearsals, advertising, or booking a theatre.

> No part of this book may be reproduced, stored in a retrieval system, or transmitted in any form, by any means, now known or yet to be invented, including mechanical, electronic, photocopying, recording, videotaping, or otherwise, without the prior written permission of the publisher.

MUSIC USE NOTE

Licensees are solely responsible for obtaining formal written permission from copyright owners to use copyrighted music in the performance of this play and are strongly cautioned to do so. If no such permission is obtained by the licensee, then the licensee must use only original music that the licensee owns and controls. Licensees are solely responsible and liable for all music clearances and shall indemnify the copyright owners of the play and their licensing agent, Samuel French, Inc., against any costs, expenses, losses and liabilities arising from the use of music by licensees.

IMPORTANT BILLING AND CREDIT REQUIREMENTS

All producers of *CLARENCE DARROW'S LAST TRIAL must* give credit to the Author of the Play in all programs distributed in connection with performances of the Play, and in all instances in which the title of the Play appears for the purposes of advertising, publicizing or otherwise exploiting the Play and/or a production. The name of the Author *must* appear on a separate line on which no other name appears, immediately following the title and *must* appear in size of type not less than fifty percent of the size of the title type.

CLARENCE DARROW'S LAST TRIAL was first produced by the New Theatre (Rafael de Acha, artistic director/Eileen Suarez, managing director) in Coral Gables, Florida on January 21, 2005. The performance was directed by Rafael de Acha, with sets by Rich Simone, costumes by Estewla Vrancovich, sound design by M. Anthony Reimer, and lighting by Michael Foster. The production stage manager was Joseph M. NeSmith. The cast was as follows:

CLARENCE DARROW	John Felix
RUBY DARROW	Susan Dempsey
LIEUTENANT JOHN RAMSEY	John Bixler
THEODORA RAMSEY	Jenny Levine
TOM LOU	Ricky J. Martinez
MRS. MONTEGU	Angie Radosh
DR. DAVID STEIN	Bill Schwartz
NANILOA WHITEFIELD CHAN	Tara Vodihn

CHARACTERS
(in order of appearance)

CLARENCE DARROW – 70s. Tall, craggy, American looks. Wears red galluses, string tie, white shirt, crumpled gray linen suit, hat of the era. Rambunctious, strong, brilliant, egocentric, stubborn, but in his seniority, aging, at an extremely vulnerable time in his life and career.

RUBY DARROW – Middle-aged. Younger than Darrow. This is a second marriage for Darrow. Ruby was his secretary. They are deeply in love. She is totally devoted to him and his work. They are partners in work; she is intuitive about him and his strengths and she trusts her opinion. More now that he's older. She believes in the causes he fights as much as he does. All he does: his triumphs, his defeats are hers too. In this way they are truly "one." She has an inner and outer beauty, is very bright, steady and intuitive. Simple print dress of the period, small heels, hat, chenille robe at start.

LIEUTENANT JOHN RAMSEY – Late 20s. Handsome. "All American" in looks and manner. A Naval officer, first Lieutenant, who bears himself as such. Sense of authority, in control of himself and others. Perhaps too much? Speaks with Southern accent.

DR. DAVID STEIN – Middle aged. Dark, Jewish. Wears vest, doctors white coat, glasses/pince-nez),smokes pipe. Man of intelligence,an avant guard doctor in the new field of psychiatry, coming into vogue at time of play. Has known Darrow since he was still in Residency and testified and helped him with the Leopold Loeb case, "Insanity as mitigating circumstance in the defense."

REPORTER TOM LOU – 30s. Asian/white/mixed blood. An ambitious, bright, assertive man with depth, perception, humor. Wears mix of Hawaiian/American/Asian clothes. A straw hat of some sort.

MRS. MONTEGU – 40-ish. Lieutenant Ramsey's mother-in-law; Theodie Ramsey's mother. Very aristocratic. WASP, Southern accent. A Southern matriarch from an old Southern plantation family in Atlanta that's kept its wealth. A heritage she's proud of. Charming, grand in manner, a great hostess, especially at Oyster Bay, L.I., their summer residence. Attractive. Seductive with men in her Southern way. Underneath is steel. Silk dress of the period, pearls, small heels.

THEODORA (THEODIE) RAMSEY – Very early 20s. Lieutenant Ramsey's wife, and Mrs. Montegu's daughter. Aristocratic, elegant WASP: blonde, attractive. Southern accent. A little of the "20's flapper" and "Southern flirt." A bubbly, "little girl" aura. People view her as slightly eccentric with dramatic flair but omething about her hints that she's been badly wounded, long ago. Wears long chartreuse chiffon scarf around neck that trails down.

NANILOA WHITEFIELD CHAN – 30s. The prosecuting attorney. Mixed blood: white, Chinese, and from a Royal Hawaiian Ali'i family. Bears herself as such. Extremely intelligent, strong, regal. A freethinker. Beautiful and passionate. Wears dark crepe dress of the period, and a Hawaiian lei.

It may be possible to double cast some of the roles.

PLAYWRIGHT'S NOTES

THE LAST TRIAL OF CLARENCE DARROW is inspired by the last major criminal court trial Clarence Darrow fought. But the play and characters are fictional except for Clarence and Ruby Darrow.

The play is a style piece. All design elements conform to this. Abstracted, suggested, part for the whole. Nothing in the text should be illustrated or literally rendered from the design standpoint. The play can adapt to a simple or a more formal, elaborate design concept. Use of a unit set with platforms, lights, sound, music, scrims, film clips and other visuals indicated in the script are an effort to suggest stylistically how changes of times, place, and ambience might be implemented on the stage. The suggestions can be simplified or amplified. There should be a sense of transience, of swirling movement, then stops, then movement again – as if the characters and the telling of their story are caught for critical moments in the glare of the light of history.

The Research and The External Services Department at the University of Hawaii at Manoa, Honolulu, Hawaii; the Research Library at the William S. Richardson Law School of the University of Hawaii, Honolulu; and the Research Departments of both the Law School Library and the Bobst Library of New York Uviversity have been of invaluable help in the research phases of this project.

THE PLACES of the play are in Chicago and the Territory of Hawaii.

THE TIME is 1931 and onwards…the very dawn of celebrity as the Lindbergh Baby is kidnapped – and it is the dawn of technology; – phones, radios – with immediate international communication and transient, fluid movement throughout the world – as World War II looms ahead…

To the indigenous peoples of Hawaii.

ACT ONE

(Abstracted sounds of railroad station: train whistles, chugging train wheels. Shadowy – isolated feeling. Swirl of smoke as if billowing from trains. Now, as if caught in spot searchlight, a man, 70ish, enters. Stooped, weary, He wears 30's fedora hat, carries overcoat, briefcase. This is **CLARENCE DARROW**. *He goes to a phone booth, and makes a call. This should not be realistic. Once phone call convention is established, characters do not hold receivers but directly speak to each other as if in same room.)*

DARROW. *(as if calling out to her in the room:)* Rube?

(Lights up on **RUBY DARROW**, *woken up, wrapping robe on as she enters room, answers phone, then looks at* **DARROW** *as if they were in same room. Scene plays as such.)*

RUBY. Dee?

DARROW. I'm out of the case, Rube.

(sounds of train station)

CAN YOU HEAR? FORCED OUT! THE SCOTTSBORO CASE!

RUBY. You still there?

STATION MASTER. *(V.O.)* NASHVILLE, LOUISVILLE, CHICAGO! NOW BOARDING, TRACK FIVE!

DARROW. THE TRAIN STATION DOWN HERE.

(talks louder)

TAKIN' THE CHICAGO SLEEPER HOME! BE THERE 8 A.M.

RUBY. What happened, Dee?

*(More train sounds: whistles, wheels chugging, **DARROW** talking louder and louder.)*

DARROW. COMMUNIST LAWYERS FROM NEW YORK GOT A STRANGLEHOLD ON THE CASE.

RUBY. CAN HARDLY HEAR YOU! WHAT?

DARROW. "Scottsboro Boys're represented by *us* now!" They said. "But always an honor to have *you*, Mr. Darrow – if you can get rid of that NAACP who sent you. Just *assist us* instead!" "ASSIST?" says I. Good naturedly, mind you. "Nine colored boys from Scottsboro accused of gang raping two white girls? Why that's my very cup of Lipton Tea, boys," says I.

RUBY. You're out of the case? Oh Lord!

DARROW. But I was calm at that point, Rube. I was *calm*! "You know though, boys, I did 'the' break-through racial rape case in this nation! First time a colored man convicted of raping a white woman got life instead of death."

RUBY. I'm so sorry Dee – they wanted you to *assist?*

DARROW. "Isaac Bond! Chicago, 1906!" says I. "Remember it by any chance, boys? Annals of American history – law schools – journals – encyclopedias, boys?" But they're sitting there, Rube, lookin twelve years old – starin' at me like I was some kinda jackass talkin about defendin' Micky Mouse!

(She turns away from facing him: he is nearly overcome with grief at this point:)

So then – then, Rube?

(She turns back to him.)

RUBY. I'm here, Dee. Little hard to hear though.

DARROW. I – I gave 'em the highlight of that Landmak Plea then:

(He launches into speech as if in courtroom.)

"If a human life is worth anything, it is worth saving!"

RUBY. Anybody at the station with you, Dee?

DARROW. What are you talkin about? You aren't listenin bird one!

(He hangs up, picks up cases moving into shadows as suddenly camera flashes. **DARROW** *whirls around, startled, as camera flashes again.* **DARROW** *looks enraged as flash goes off again and again.)*

Get that damn thing away from me will you?

*(***DARROW*** exits. Lights up on corner of ***DARROW****'s Chicago apartment living room. Humble. Sparse. Gray winter morning with falling snow seen through window overlooking Lake Michigan.* ***DARROW****'s wicker rocker by window. Frayed reddish rug. Bookcase with books overflowing onto the floor.* ***RUBY*** *at table, filling pen from inkpot, then writing in large ledger checkbook open before her.)*

RUBY. *(reading:)* "Pay to the Order of"

(writing:) Horace Baylor, M.D. –

*(***DARROW*** *bursts into room brandishing newspaper.)*

DARROW. RUBY!!

RUBY. I'm right here, dear – you get a little sleep on the train?

(She rises to embrace him but he charges past her into room.)

DARROW. See this? They caught me at the train station.

(He brandishes paper.)

"*DARROW DISMISSED*"! Mug shot a mile high. Like a mad dog, Ruby! Like a –

RUBY. Stop! You'll make yourself sick!

(She takes paper from him, tries to take off his coat. He pulls away from her.)

DARROW. Why don't they print the truth? "FORCED OUT"! Asked for their $1000 retainer back too – I tell you that? And there's no $5000 fee of course...

(She turns away, shocked, angry, frustrated.)

What's wrong?

RUBY. The 1000's gone! Back rent – grocery bills for two months – electric –

(She looks down at ledger.)

And Dr. Baylor? I swore to him: "The $800 for that surgery will be –"

(She stops short.)

Well we'll pay it off. Don't worry. Look – it's The Depression – everybody's in debt…

(She detaches check from ledger.)

DARROW. *Pro bono* all my life! And now? Seventy-six years old for cryin' out loud. And I can't pay my doctor bill!!

RUBY. Dee, don't do that to yourself!

DARROW. Scottsboro would've solved it all! Money – colored boys free – my legacy like a rock!

(He is imagining this scene as he speaks:)

Old warrior, high in the saddle – ridin' off –

RUBY. *(softly laughing, amused)* Ole Cowhand Dee?

DARROW. You think it's *funny?* My hat's on the *hook*, Ruby! I am yesterday's newspaper!

(He takes newspaper, tearing it up. She's gone back to check book, adding up figures. He notices, takes checkbook, tearing it up too.)

Not in *front* of me!

(He goes to sideboard, pours whiskey shot, downs it. She goes there, shoves whisky decanter into sideboard cupboard slams door.)

RUBY. Well, not in front of *me!*

(He looks at her, gets idea, starts rummaging through his books, pulling one out, putting it in briefcase.)

DARROW. There's one!

RUBY. Now what's that for?

DARROW. The appraiser.

RUBY. Appraiser?

DARROW. Gonna sell all these autographed books. Pay off Dr. Baylor, and everybody else! Just decided: I'm sellin off my office desk, chairs, bookcases, lamps, sign on the door too! Givin up the damn office. Why the hell pay rent two places when I can work here.

(He's trying to jam several books in his small briefcase. They don't fit. She fills pen again, secures cap on ink bottle, smoothes ledger pages, then closes it. Begins writing figures on pad again.)

RUBY. *(casually:)* Chester called.

DARROW. Chester Hawthorne? Here?

RUBY. From New York. His law office.

DARROW. *(sarcastically)* Condolence call for Scottsboro? Saw my puss in *The New York Times*?

RUBY. He –

DARROW. *(interrupting:)* So damn smug since he left here! Deeper the Depression, deeper the pockets of "Wall Street Chester, Ink!"

RUBY. Chester's your good friend, Dee. You two travel back very far in time.

DARROW. A forgotten time! 'Cause he travels now with hoity-toity New York tycoons.

RUBY. *(casually)* He'll be calling back.

DARROW. To gloat?

RUBY. Wants you to reconsider that Hawaiian case. That family in Hawaii doesn't want to use their Honolulu lawyers for their Defense.

DARROW. HAWAII? Christ, I turned that down a while ago. And down it *stays*! It's *his* client's family up on the murder charge in Hawaii. That's why he called.

(He's trying books one way then another, packing repacking.)

RUBY. He said he thinks the trial could be "an historical moment in time" for you, Dee – if it was argued right.

DARROW. "Historical moment in time"? Every moment's historical in time. What the hell's he mean by that?

RUBY. The International spotlight'll be on the trial is what he meant. "They're broadcasting live from the courtroom all around the world first time in history!" He said. Reporters from Le Monde – Der Berliner – The London Times. "Clarence would be centerstage again with a significant case" is what he meant.

(She is adding numbers, figuring their balance.)

DARROW. Centerstage wrong side! There're race issues. I can't touch that case with a 10 foot pole. And we went over and over that already. Don't you remember? How can I begin to defend white rich aristocrats in Honolulu for killing a Hawaiian??

RUBY. They're rich all right…they…they're offering you a fortune – $30,000 fee, Chester said – lodgings at the Royal Hawaiian Hotel – and a stateroom on a fancy boat to cruise down there in. If you can imagine us "cruising"!

*(**DARROW** looks at her. They both smile a little. She goes back to adding figures, he keeps looking at her. Then:)*

DARROW. Somethin like that trip'd be milk and honey for you though, huh?

(He chucks her under chin.)

Puttin' up with me all these years for God's sake!

RUBY. Trip'd be a treat for anybody. Have to be a fool not to relish something like that. But it's not the reason to go, Dee…for us.

(She looks around room.)

Depression Times or not, we're both pretty used to how we live, huh – so you can do what you do. Reason to go would be: the case is right for you.

DARROW. Well, it's not.

(beat)

RUBY. Chester did remind me you'd felt the family was probably innocent – when you considered it before – from all the documents – papers – everything else he and the Honolulu lawyers sent –

DARROW. Damn it, I know they're innocent. And you know that's not why I turned it down.

RUBY. But then too, you had the choice of Scottsboro at that time.

(He turns away.)

Maybe you should just rethink a little? Remember?

(He turns back, looks at her.)

A naval Lieutenant's wife's gang raped by Hawaiian thugs – but then at the trial –

DARROW. *(interrupting, remembering)* The jury splits on racial lines. 5/7 wasn't it?

RUBY. Five orientals to acquit. Seven whites to convict...as I recall...

(They are both getting caught up in story:)

DARROW. They cannot reach a verdict! One hundred hours of deliberation! The bailiff reporting shouting, yelling in the jury room – and they simply cannot reach a verdict!

RUBY. So the judge declares a mistrial and –

DARROW. *(jumping in)* The Hawaiians go on probation. Until the retrial. Scared for their lives. And then –

RUBY. *(jumping in)* The D.A. tells the family: "the Hawaiian gang leader just sent word" –

DARROW. Privately – discretely –

RUBY. Before the case comes to trial again – he wants to sign a confession – for a plea bargain that –

DARROW. *(jumping in)* Secretly – so his gang doesn't know –

RUBY. In the family's house –

DARROW. Where the Hawaiian's gonna turn on his gang. Then –

RUBY. *(jumping in)* He turns on the *family* instead – with a knife!

DARROW. And then – the family shoots *him* in defense instead!

RUBY. "Highly intriguing case"! Chester reminded me that those were your exact words when –

(Phone rings.)

Oh, I bet that's him –

DARROW. Let it ring.

(Phone rings again.)

RUBY. I told him you'd be home by now.

DARROW. Tell him I left.

(He starts off. **RUBY** *speaking looking at person:)*

RUBY. Hello?

(Spot on **RAMSEY** *looking at her from faraway area. They speak loudly.)*

RAMSEY. Is this the Darrow Residence, ma'am?

*(***DARROW** *stops, turns, looks at him.)*

RUBY. Yes. This is Mrs. Darrow.

RAMSEY. Honor, ma'am. Lt. John Ramsey here. From Pearl Harbor? Our family's legal counsellor in New York – Chester Hawthorne?

RUBY. Yes?

RAMSEY. I told him I wanted to call myself. Plead my case to Mr. Darrow directly. If I might speak with him, please, ma'am?

RUBY. Dee – Hawaii! The Lieutenant!

(to **RAMSEY***)*

Just a minute, please? Here's Clarence Darrow now!

(She pushes phone into **DARROW***'s hand.* **DARROW** *throws her a look.)*

RAMSEY. Mr. Darrow, sir?

*(***DARROW** *reluctantly joins conversation.)*

DARROW. Yes?

RAMSEY. Privilege, sir. Lt. John Ramsey, here. My wife's the one got assaulted down here – and now her mother and I are accused of murdering the gang leader and –

DARROW. I know all about it, Lieutenant. But I'm afraid I'm gonna have to turn your case down again. I'm sorry.

RAMSEY. Good God, you don't think we're guilty, sir?

DARROW. Look, son – I think you were most probably tricked by a Hawaiian thug who almost murdered you all! It's just I'm not so good unless I'm fighting for the underdog –

RAMSEY. But you saved Leopold and Loeb! They were white, wealthy – and guilty! And their victim was a child!

DARROW. Everyone there was white and wealthy: victim. Leopold. Loeb. Anyhow what saved 'em was I argued they were mentally unstable.

(A beat. Two. Then:)

RAMSEY. Oh?

DARROW. Pleaded 'em guilty of murder then brought temporary insanity in as cause…mitigating circumstance. Let me open the door a little more to insanity as a legitimate plea! God, I loved that chance!

(beat)

RAMSEY. Of course –

DARROW. Your Honolulu lawyers'll do a good job for you all, I'm sure. And I wish you all the luck –

RAMSEY. *(interrupting)* Mr. Darrow? Listen? Please? Local lawyers here aren't good. First trial my wife was even given a bad prosecutor from the D.A.'s office! Incriminating evidence tainted, botched, suppressed – critical witnesses not called. That mistrial was because of that, sir. Not racial top dog/under dog issues. Good lawyers and we'd've won.

(beat)

DARROW. Be that as it may, I –

RAMSEY. *(interrupting:)* My mother-in-law's life and mine are on the line down here, sir – we're desperate –

DARROW. I just can't!

(A beat. Then two.)

RAMSEY. Look, Mr. Darrow – I panicked and blanked when he pulled his knife and said he'd rape my wife again! I went crazy! Wild in the moment – shooting crazy wild – an accident that I shot him –

*(He looks at **DARROW**.)*

We wanted him brought justice legally! That's what inviting him to the villa to sign the confession was about!

*(A long silence: **DARROW**'s thinking of something.)*

DARROW. That ever happen to you before, son?

RAMSEY. What?

DARROW. "Blanking"? "Panicking" – Going "crazy wild in the moment"?

(beat, then softly)

RAMSEY. I've blanked before…lost time…after my wife Theodie was…assaulted…and –

DARROW. What?

(RAMSEY *looks around to see if he's being overheard. Then a whisper:)*

RAMSEY. Happened on the submarine I command too. After my wife's assault – I pretended a migraine – was relieved of duty—

(again a lengthy silence)

DARROW. See a doctor, son?

RAMSEY. *(ashamed)* Private psychiatrist –

DARROW. Have trouble like this – before Hawaii?

(Silence. Then:)

RAMSEY. Annapolis –

DARROW. What happened there?

RAMSEY. Couldn't separate what was happening from what I thought was happening – ended up in the infirmary –

(long beat)

DARROW. When did you say the trial starts?

RAMSEY. Five weeks –

DARROW. Wouldn't give a lawyer time enough to tie his shoe! Takes a week to get down there, doesn't it?

RAMSEY. You're thinking about coming? Oh my God

DARROW. Thinking about – just thinking –

RAMSEY. Look – the Honolulu lawyers have done all the ground work already and Chester will send you the whole background of the first case – you'd have every possible kind of help. Oh my God, Mr. Darrow! There's a chance?

DARROW. Get all your medical records to me fast as you can. Don't forget Annapolis.

RAMSEY. Yes sir –

DARROW. If I came – *if* I came – I'd be coming for the chance to go for a temporary insanity plea, Lieutenant. Highly experimental –

RAMSEY. I – I see –

DARROW. You willing to take the stand on that plea, son?

RAMSEY. I – I – what's the risk?

DARROW. Reputation – career – all that –

RAMSEY. I – I – yes…

DARROW. I'd need to see a psychiatrist friend of mine, first. Helped me with Leopold and Loeb.

(Blackout on **RAMSEY.** **DARROW** *to* **RUBY***:)*

Call David at Chicago Psychiatric, will you Rube?

(He puts on hat.)

Let him know what I'm thinking of doin?

(Starts walking. Over should to **RUBY***:)*

Should be there by noon—tell him I want his advice –

(Blackout on **RUBY.** *Lights up,* **STEIN** *'s office.* **DARROW** *walks in.* **STEIN** *reading from a medical book. He rises.)*

STEIN. Clarence!

(They shake hands.)

DARROW. Ruby called?

STEIN. I think there's a damn good shot with this, Clarence.

(Several beats. **DARROW** *mulling this over, smiles at* **STEIN**.*)*

DARROW. Would you come testify to that, David?

(beat)

STEIN. Other side of the world, Clarence...just lost my best resident – there're good psychiatrists there, Clarence – I don't think –

DARROW. Trust some Local Yokel? I never would've saved Leopold or Loeb without you on board. I need you, David – your experience – credentials. If we get this plea established? Might help you start your own clinic – like that Karl Meninger friend of yours has –

STEIN. And wouldn't I like that.

(beat)

DARROW. Well?

STEIN. I – I'll try to come –

DARROW. What the hell kind of answer is that? TRY?

*(***DARROW*** starts from area.)*

STEIN. Clarence? Count me in!

(Blackout on **STEIN***, as* **DARROW** *enters his home area, sitting, thinking.)*

DARROW. Ruby?

*(***RUBY*** enters, studying him a moment, then:)*

RUBY. Stein's agreed and you're taking the case!

DARROW. I am.

RUBY. Not worried about the race issues like you were before then?

DARROW. Mental illness is universal, Rube. I'll cross all color lines with a plea like this.

(He is pacing, thinking.)

RUBY. Maybe I'm playing devil's advocate now – but there are race issues – natives who don't want us there taking over their people – their language – their land…

(He continues thinking, not really listening.)

And the Lieutenant's being Navy? Sailing their waters every day he goes to work. All of it could work itself into the trial, you said – you felt that pretty strongly before, Dee –

DARROW. I don't think it anymore, all right? It's like Chester said before:

(pacing again, thinking)

Times change…Hawaiians're Americans now – thousands of new jobs, schools – medical system we got going. Democratic legal system we helped set up…why the Lieutenant's part of *their* Navy, Rube! Risking *his* life protecting *them*!

(He stops a minute.)

RUBY. But the race issue's are still there, aren't they? They –

DARROW. *(interrupting)* Christ, I want to go! I've got the chance to establish a new plea. At my age, for God's sake. "Temporary Insanity." I'll put my name on it – establish it in the courts. Make good come out of this trial for the future. So what if there's a little hostility around? Think I haven't handled that before in trial? God, it's in my bones to go now, Rube! In my bones!

(He starts pacing again. Then:)

I'm gonna ask for a signed agreement from the family before I accept. Hardly ever done but I'm in a position to ask for it and get it! Powerful people like this? A fella has to protect himself every step.

(paces, thinking)

Get this down?

(She get pen, paper, starts writing.)

DARROW. *(cont.)* "It is agreed Clarence Darrow will control all trial decisions – including but not exclusive to choices of jurors, witnesses and nature of their testimony. And he shall control including but not exclusive to all pleas, strategies, appeals – before, during and after trial." We'll fill in more details later.

RUBY. Then the trip is on?

DARROW. They give me that power and control in writing? The trip is on.

(Lights change. A bright, clear, sunny day. In distance, Hawaiian music, which grows louder as we see on scrim: film of harbor, girls hulaing. Sounds of people who've gathered to meet boat. Very festive atmosphere. Music loud. **DARROW** *comes down boat ramp docked in harbor, wearing lei. Applause, cheers.* **REPORTER** *appears: Flash of his camera.)*

REPORTER. *(calling:)* Aloha! Couple more photos, sir?

(Camera flashes again. Sounds of people. Other flashes popping all around as though other photographers are there.)

Care to give us your opening statement about coming to Hawaii, sir?

DARROW. *(looking around)* Outstanding scenery: those Hula girls over there, huh? Uh, the palm trees! The palm trees is what I meant.

(All laugh.)

REPORTER. Care to comment on the case, sir?

DARROW. We've had a whole winter in Chicago struggling with 18 below, nine inches of snow…weather's wonderful here! So I sure hope my wife brought my summer suit for court. She's already in the car that's waiting –

(He waves toward car, starts to move, **REPORTER** *snaps shot of* **DARROW**, *then blocks him.)*

Guess I'll just go on over there and ask her. If you'll excuse me?

*(He waves toward car, tries to go but **REPORTER** keeps blocking. Scene takes on "stop/start" quality.)*

REPORTER. Have you decided on a "Code of Honor" Plea? "The Unwritten Law" as it's sometimes called. It's what the family wants, we hear – "Code of Honor" – "Unwritten Law"?

DARROW. I always aim to please – so I just may have decided on that plea. I just may have!

REPORTER. It's what we hear in the native neighborhoods too –

DARROW. You represent some native paper?

REPORTER. Yes sir: Honolulu Sun!

DARROW. *(smiling)* Native newspapers are the ones with the real beat on the news. Don't want anything to get around of course – about a Code of Honor plea –

REPORTER. We don't want that plea! Natives, I mean. Hoping you won't go with it, sir – "that a person can take the law into their own hands if they can't get justice in the courts"? That's a posse. Spells trouble for the natives, sir.

DARROW. *(waving to **RUBY** in waiting car)* We sure don't want trouble. We sure don't!

*(He starts walking to new area, as simultaneously, lights up on incarceration boat at Pearl Harbor, **RAMSEY** pacing on deck. As **DARROW** walks to area, up gangplank ramp:)*

RAMSEY. *(waving, calling down)* Hallooo down there!

*(**DARROW** looks up, waves back.)*

Welcome to Pearl Harbor – Mr. Darrow?

*(**DARROW** comes onto deck.)*

Honor, sir!

(They shake hands.)

DARROW. Lieutenant!

RAMSEY. So glad to meet you in person, sir. Here – here, this way – so appreciate your coming to Pearl Harbor so soon too.

(He's leading them to cabin lounge area, **DARROW** *looking around.)*

Just an old navy incarceration boat –

(They enter cabin lounge area.)

Here – sit – make yourself comfortable, sir –

(They sit. **DARROW** *offers cigarette.)*

DARROW. Smoke?

RAMSEY. Thank you, sir.

(They light up.)

So grateful you've taken us on, sir.

DARROW. You know how much I sympathize with all your family's been through.

RAMSEY. We know it's a high risk case for you, sir – pleading for people like us.

DARROW. Gonna knock everybody's socks off with that plea, son. I –

*(***MRS. MONTEGU*** *makes a grand entrance.* **THEODIE** *with her. The* **MEN** *stand.* **MRS. MONTEGU** *offers hand to* **DARROW.***)*

MRS. MONTEGU. My dear Mr. Darrow.

RAMSEY. My wife's mother, Mrs. Montegu.

DARROW. Honor to meet you, Mrs. Montegu.

MRS. MONTEGU. The honor is mine!

DARROW. Chester Hawthorne? Spoke to him before we sailed – he sends regards.

MRS. MONTEGU. Dear Chester! My daughter, Mr. Darrow? Theodie Montegu-Ramsey.

THEODIE. *(shaking his hand)* Mr. Darrow –

DARROW. And Chester's daughter, Bunny, sends regards to you, Mrs. Ramsey.

THEODIE. Bunny Hawthorne? My stars, I went to boarding school with old Bunny Hawthorne!

MRS. MONTEGU. And regards to Mrs. Darrow. Please tell her I trust the stateroom on the boat and the suite at the Royal Hawaiian were reasonable choices.

DARROW. Excellent choices! She loves it all!

MRS. MONTEGU. Because in spite of everything, we so want you to have some enjoyment – in your free hours. As best you can.

DARROW. Always love to enjoy myself, madam! In my free hours – as best I can.

(He smiles at her. Everyone laughs.)

MRS. MONTEGU. Well? Let's sit! Sit! Everybody sit!

(They do.)

You know, Mr. Darrow, Claudine Durham wants to give a little party in your honor? At the Oahu Club? She'll want you to say a few words. "Lionizing the Lion," she's calling her evening – if you're "game"?

DARROW. "Lionizing the Lion?"

(He roars, imitating lion. They all laugh.)

I'm "game." You see? I'm fair "game."

(They laugh, more.)

MRS. MONTEGU. You are too funny Mr. Darrow. –

DARROW. *(immediately rising to occasion, rising:)* I'll say something light!

(as if at dinner a dinner table)

"Folks," I'll say…I'm gonna call 'em "folks"…

MRS. MONTEGU. Claudine will simply adore that!

DARROW. "I've got thirty-seven pair of gallowses!" I'll say, "Different colors and I brought 'em all along!" Then I'll open my jacket –

(He opens jacket, displaying pair of bright-red suspenders. Hooks his thumb in them. They laugh.)

I'll be wearin' two, three pairs though. Oughta get me a laugh.

MRS. MONTEGU. A positive hoot! A veritable "lion's roar!" She's a Pineapple Durham, of course.

DARROW. *(chuckling, bewildered)* Pineapple Durham?

THEODIE. *(laughing lightly)* Mummer means the Durham's grow pineapples. And practically own Hawaii!

MRS. MONTEGU. I do wish I could be there. But neither Johnny nor I can leave this boat incarceration – of all the silly things! Admiral's said he'll accompany Mrs. Darrow though. And Theodie, maybe, you'll let Mr. Darrow escort you?

THEODIE. I once did a wicked Charleston, Mr. Darrow. Top of the table? But Johnny said:

(imitating **RAMSEY***:)*

"Conduct unbecoming an officer's wife!"

(She salutes, giggles, rearranging scarf. **RAMSEY** *goes to her good-naturedly, arm around her shoulder.)*

RAMSEY. If you want to Charleston with Mr. Darrow, sweetheart, I'd be delighted!

MRS. MONTEGU. Well then – let's ring for coffee?

(She rings bell.)

Their Kona beans, Mr. Darrow, make a tantalizing brew.

DARROW. Thanks, but...but a little hot for coffee, ma'am.

MRS. MONTEGU. Oh, I do wish we had a more warm weather refreshment to offer you as we have in our summer home – in Oyster Bay? Something minty, lemony. We are in such reduced circumstances, as you will understand dear Mr. Darrow, imprisoned on this boat. Still it is a mercy the Navy could arrange even this – spared us that sordid Honolulu jail at least!

(a beat)

THEODIE. Mr. Darrow?

DARROW. Ma'am?

THEODIE. I wanted you to know the very thought of testifying again makes me about to swoon, Mr. Darrow...

DARROW. Look, ma'am, I'm gonna try my best to make all this suffering only a dim memory for everybody.

THEODIE. Oh, please God!

DARROW. Let me tell you what I'm plannin' then? I know the law here's "one innocent, all innocent" – so I'm figurin' to just to plead the Lieutenant, because he has cause and motivation. Not gonna put anyone else on the stand at all.

THEODIE. Answer to a young girl's prayers, sir.

MRS. MONTEGU. I won't have to take the stand then either, Mr. Darrow.

DARROW. No ma'am.

MRS. MONTEGU. Oh thank heaven! Because I do feel so hideously responsible, Mr. Darrow – Johnny was in no state, you see – so I drove. If only I'd taken the other turn at that intersection – Kalani might've lived! I keep going over and over it all in my mind 'til I feel about to burst, Mr. Darrow.

RAMSEY. Kalani's the Hawaiian.

DARROW. Yes, I know.

MRS. MONTEGU. You see – that mountain Villa I rented is so far out from the Honolulu Hospital – and I was going at such breakneck speed to get Kalani there – and was such a stranger to the roads – I turned left instead of right. And suddenly we were on the cliff road!

RAMSEY. Where they stopped us for speeding – found Kalani not breathing. And – arrested us!

MRS. MONTEGU. I get shaky even talking about it, Mr. Darrow.

DARROW. I give my word neither you or your daughter will have to relive this on the stand!

MRS. MONTEGU. Thank God you've come!

(**DARROW** *opens briefcase.*)

DARROW. As to the plea? Let me over just a few of the facts tonight. The Lieutenant –

RAMSEY. Please call me Johnny, sir.

DARROW. *(smiling)* Johnny. You had been under cruel and unusual mental strain before the incident at the Villa. For how long would you say?

RAMSEY. Close to five months. Theodie's injuries were so severe – and Mother M. was under such tremendous stress – coming down here to nurse Theodie all the way from Atlanta! I bore the brunt myself…like anyone would, sir.

MRS. MONTEGU. Theodie was in the most hideous pain, Mr. Darrow. Only sipping through a straw – jaws wired together from the beating…

RAMSEY. And – then – she had to undergo a curretage from the assaults. She'd become pregnant along with everything else. Complications followed – we – we don't know if we can even have children. We –

THEODIE. Johnny –

*(**THEODIE** takes **RAMSEY**'s hand. A beat.)*

DARROW. And all the while commanding a submarine, Johnny? Responsible every minute down there for the whole crew? You told me you were at the breaking point…how long would you estimate you stayed there?

THEODIE. Johnny started not to be himself the minute I was assaulted.

DARROW. From that time on you started seeing the local psychiatrist?

MRS. MONTEGU. What?

DARROW. I'd better ask him to have his appointment book ready with all dates –

*(**DARROW** makes a note of this.)*

MRS. MONTEGU. Psychiatrist's records?

DARROW. For the temporary insanity plea. Hasn't Johnny told you?

MRS. MONTEGU. No!

RAMSEY. I thought you'd want to present the plea to everyone, sir.

(beat; smiling:)

MRS. MONTEGU. But Johnny's the most steadfast man on earth, Mr. Darrow. Anyone would be a bit trembly with what he went through!

DARROW. Fortunately past records reveal more than "trembling," ma'am.

MRS. MONTEGU. Fortunately?

DARROW. Annapolis to start…

MRS. MONTEGU. Ancient history! Buried deep in the sands of time!

DARROW. Lord, I don't want it buried!

(beat)

MRS. MONTEGU. Well, of course, you're the best judge – but a temporary insanity plea? Extremely damaging! We are a military family, you see. And we have confidence Johnny has a brilliant future ahead in the Navy – once we get past this.

RAMSEY. Please, Mother M., I –

MRS. MONTEGU. Don't be shy Johnny, for Lord's sake! He's already commander of a submarine here, Mr. Darrow. Our newest, most dangerous military weapon – as you may know. Why, a plea like this would simply destroy his climb to the top. To say nothing of wrecking our family name!

THEODIE. Mummer!

MRS. MONTEGU. Theodie, hush! We are looking for a Code of Honor plea, Mr. Darrow.

JOHNNY. Mother M. I –

MRS. MONTEGU. Johnny? Please! Well then – Mr. Darrow – I'd thought you'd indicated that plea in the local papers. I'd actually planned discussing it tonight. My husband, the Colonel, wants it. The Admiral here at Pearl wants it, the local team of lawyers wants it – and a great many of our Naval and American community on the islands want it too. You see, it would give Johnny the right to take the law in his own hands if he couldn't get justice and –

DARROW. *(interrupting)* Never! I spread it around the papers for strategy – that's all!

MRS. MONTEGU. But my dear Mr. Darrow –

DARROW. Your husband – the Colonel – signed the agreement putting all decisions in my hands. I'm hoping to establish temporary insanity in the courts with this case.

MRS. MONTEGU. *(aghast)* Our case?

DARROW. Bring an expert witness down here, if you'll agree to his fee. Steep but worth it. Dr. David Stein. Brilliant Psychiatrist.

MRS. MONTEGU. *(managing a week little laugh)* An expert – at our expense – to "certify" to the world Johnny's insane? You either must be joking – or a bit overcome with our tropical heat?

DARROW. Like I said – we agreed – in writing – all the legal decisions are mine.

MRS. MONTEGU. We all didn't *really* agree to anything, Mr. Darrow. You see, down here in this territory – end of the world – words on paper are very cheaply bought and sold.

DARROW. *(looking at her sharply:)* Not my words!

MRS. MONTEGU. Admiral would simply blanch at the very idea of his commanding officer declared insane in court – and he's so very influential –

DARROW. *(interrupting)* Admiral's not on trial for his life, ma'am – you are!

MRS. MONTEGU. The Colonel's a very –

DARROW. And the Colonel's not the defense lawyer, ma'am – I am! Don't any of 'em know how much trouble you folks are in? There's a powerful circumstantial case against you, Mrs. Montegu.

MRS. MONTEGU. They haven't got one witness to what happened!

RAMSEY. Mother M.? Listen to Mr. Darrow. Please!

DARROW. The dead body was in the back seat when your car was stopped. Both of you in front – a bullet in Kalani from your gun – found in your Villa – with yours and Johnny's prints.

MRS. MONTEGU. We all know Johnny handled it and it was *my* gun – but purchased months ago. I was just so terrified staying alone up there in the mountains!

DARROW. Johnny pulled the trigger – left his prints. The rest is only your word – and you told me just now how "words are cheap" down here!

MRS. MONTEGU. *(rising)* I'm afraid I've become dreadfully unnerved by all of this! In pieces, to be honest. I simply cannot discuss any of this a moment more – so – if you'll excuse me?

(She starts out. RAMSEY & DARROW rise. DARROW shakes hands with her. She smiles, trying pull self together.)

Good-night? And – I trust you will think it all over, dear Mr. Darrow? So we'll all be in harmony with whatever you choose?

DARROW. Of course…

(She exits.)

Her life's on the line too, whether she acknowledges it or not! God, I wish you'd told her and got it settled before I came!

RAMSEY. I'm sorry, sir. I should've – but – well, we've just been beside ourselves –

(beat)

Look – here's a thought Mr. Darrow –

DARROW. What?

RAMSEY. Does she really have to know for sure you're going ahead with the insanity plea?

*(**THEODIE** and **RAMSEY** link eyes, extremely excited at idea of this little plot.)*

DARROW. I think so. There's the question of the psychiatrist's fee. I have to wire him $2000 right away and she's footing all the bills, isn't she?

(beat)

THEODIE. *(excited)* I have discretionary funds, Mr. Darrow. I can arrange the doctor's fee.

*(She takes **RAMSEY**'s hand.)*

RAMSEY. And I'll be prepping alone and not with her, won't I sir?

DARROW. Yes –

RAMSEY. And you agreed you wanted her in agreement with "whatever you chose."

DARROW. I guess I did –

THEODIE. Then why can't Mummer think you're reconsidering? That it's all up in the air? Daddy and the Admiral can think that too. And the local lawyers.

DARROW. I don't know – I sure don't want to lie – mislead the folks on our side –

RAMSEY. It's just postponing the telling. Not lying. Misleading.

DARROW. I – I just don't know as I'm comfortable with it though – 'specially your mother.

THEODIE. Mummer's all to pieces now and can't think straight. But that's just a temporary and unusual circumstance, Mr. Darrow.

RAMSEY. Sheltered woman. Protected life. And put through the mill with everything down here. Then the tensions tonight of meeting you. But she'll come around, for my sake and Theodie's. She always has.

THEODIE. She'll accommodate. By the time we're in trial Mummer'll be back to her old self, standing right by us. She'll manage to forget what she thought was right. She has that way about her: forgetting what she thinks is right –

*(**DARROW** shuts briefcase.)*

DARROW. So then – we start prep tomorrow in your cabin?

RAMSEY. Temporary insanity plea. Thank you, sir.

(They shake hands on it.)

THEODIE. I'll leave with you, Mr. Darrow – Johnny?

*(**THEODIE** kisses **RAMSEY** with some passion, tosses scarf over shoulder, joins **DARROW**. They walk down ramp from boat as **RAMSEY** takes out pack of cigarettes, begins to smoke, pacing on deck in nervous, almost "quick-march" step, then exits.)*

THEODIE. I come every day. Johnny likes candy so much I bring him coconut drops every time –

(They stand, she looks at him, giggling, a little mischievous.)

DARROW. I think it's worth your every effort to help him. He's a good man, ma'am.

(They start walking. Following scene occurs as they stop then walk then stop, etc.)

THEODIE. Well – I am trying to help – and don't I just know what a good man he is –

*(She fingers her scarf, looks away, starts walking ahead, **DARROW** following. Comes beside her.)*

DARROW. I felt fatherly to him right off the bat? Smart – friendly – respectful – practical! Grasps the situation completely, doesn't he?

THEODIE. Oh, he does grasps it all, Mr. Darrow. Very well.

DARROW. Gonna make me a good witness. Feel it in my bones!

THEODIE. Well, that's wonderful

DARROW. All that military discipline's gonna carry him right straight through on the stand.

(He stops walking as does she.)

You know, you just can't shake up a military man!

THEODIE. No sir, you really can't! It's carried him through everything!

*(She stares at **DARROW** then starts walking again. He follows suit.)*

DARROW. More worried about your mother. Like a vote of confidence from her 100%.

THEODIE. *(laughing)* She'll cooperate – but like everyone says – we aristocrats don't give our real confidence to anyone – except each other!

(long beat as she stops, scrutinizing him)

But I'm an exception: I give my confidence to any person I trust.

DARROW. Wonderful I can count on that!

THEODIE. I confide things? Important things?

(She changes subject.)

You know – on the boat?

DARROW. Yes?

THEODIE. I set out the candy and then play three handed bridge with them.

*(looks back at **DARROW**, then somewhat confidential:)*

Done that since I was little. Three handed bridge. My Daddy – the Colonel? He taught me.

*(She keeps focusing on **DARROW**.)*

See I was his "special girl" – only child – my – my Daddy? He – he – taught me lots of things.

(She laughs, a little hysterical? Maybe. She then begins fussing with her scarf, arranging, rearranging it.)

DARROW. I'm sure.

THEODIE. You are? Like riding his great big horse – you know about that?

(She's staring at him.)

DARROW. No – not that –

(He's studying her. She twirls her purse. They start walking.)

THEODIE. Of course not. How could you? Well, he was an expert horseman...my daddy...

DARROW. I see.

THEODIE. Roughrider. Went to Santiago with Teddy Roosevelt. Cavalry. We're distant relatives of Teddy. Daddy named me for him – Theodora.

(She smiles.)

Thomas Edison's a grand uncle. Mummer's side. They used to say: Edison side of the family is always "lit up!"

*(****DARROW**** laughs.)*

Family joke...

DARROW. Distinguished family to be proud of, Mrs. Ramsey.

(They stop and she looks at him, then nervously smiling.)

THEODIE. Father shot a bullet through the headboard of a freshman's bed at Yale. While the boy was asleep. Almost killed him.

(laughs again, nervously)

Hazing. His fraternity. They expelled him and he went on to West Point instead. Start of his brilliant military career!

*(She looks dead-on at ****DARROW****.)*

Now? He has a direct line to President Hoover!

(again her nervous laugh)

Well. All the men in the family seem to get caught for one wild, violent thing or another!

*(****DARROW**** looking at her.)*

Then?

(another nervous laugh)

They just get themselves "reinstated"...like they hadn't done anything at all.

(She laughs again. Long pause. She turns away.)

Mr. Darrow?

DARROW. Yes?

(She doesn't answer. Instead looks at her watch.)

Yes, ma'am what is it?

THEODIE. *(a new tone, glancing at watch)* It's so late – I'm never out this late in Pearl Harbor –

DARROW. Escort you back to Honolulu?

THEODIE. No – no thank you –

(She look at him again, slightly confidential.)

You see I drove the car.

DARROW. Tonight?

THEODIE. *(seems confused)* What?

DARROW. You drive alone at night now, I mean.

(beat as she looks at him)

THEODIE. Huh? Oh…oh no – not anymore! Johnny and Mummer would never let me. Tonight was the exception, Mr. Darrow – to greet you. I'll be fine – highway from Pearl's always busy…

*(She takes both **DARROW**'s hands in hers, laughs lightly and smiles.)*

Delightful meeting you, Mr. Darrow – at long last.

*(She exits. **DARROW** starts off as **REPORTER** appears. Flash of his camera shooting **DARROW**.)*

REPORTER. Evening, Mr. Darrow. Statement after visiting your clients for the first time, sir? Have you decided tonight on the unwritten law as the plea?

DARROW. Well, sir – the way I see it there are too many written laws now. A fella can't really keep track of all of 'em he's supposed to abide by. The Prohibition law for example? Makes it too darn hard for a fella to get a drink!

*(**REPORTER** laughs.)*

But I do like unwritten laws!

(DARROW exits one way, REPORTER runs to new area: corner of his office. Lights up on desk with typewriter, phone, mic. Morse code beeps. Then he types and speaks words as [possibly] they also roll across top of proscenium:)

REPORTER. "DARROW MEETS CLIENTS. HINTS STRONGLY AT UNWRITTEN LAW PLEA!"

(He continues typing as lights up: brilliant sunshine. Possibly on back scrim: shots of Waikiki Beach. Honolulu. Festive ambiance. Hawaiian and calliope music mix, possibly twirling carousel horse descending on pole while helium balloons drift on as Morse Code beeps.)

REPORTER. *(picking up text)* Good morning! Tommy Lou here at WHLU, your native news, Honolulu. April 3, 1932. And a bright and beautiful morning as the "Montegu-Ramsey Trial" begins jury selection.

(He leaves desk, begins strolling towards Courthouse area, observing the sights, speaking directly to audience.)

Downtown – a flood of world travellers – adventurers – sensation seekers. A "carnival" atmosphere taking over. They say it always happens with Mr. Darrow's mainland trials – Scopes trial particularly…but surely unexpected here –

(in Courthouse area:)

In front of The Courthouse now, folks – new telegraph lines up to radio broadcast this trial to the mainland – LIVE- an historic first! *Special passes* given to those with what they call "legitimate interests' to go in but…*barricades* up to hold back the rest of the people?

(He looks around, surprised.)

Everyone's searched for *bombs*, folks!! *Guns!* There's a fear of native hostility towards this trial! *Shocking*! But true –

(He steps closer.)

REPORTER. *(cont.)* Near the Courthouse now: desks, typewriters, telephones being hauled into courtroom for international reporters –

(DARROW enters area, looks around, REPORTER watching, moving to side where DARROW doesn't see him.)

Thirty-six years ago? The courthouse was the Hall of Chiefs – the Ali'i – our royal advisors to Queen Leliuokalani – they met here serving the *Hawaiian people*! Across the courtyard? Iolani Palace. Home of our Queen and courtiers. Now? Office of the American Governor! For "The American Territory"!

(DARROW before a statue with inscription. NANILOA enters, watching. REPORTER to audience, sadness now in voice:)

King Kamehameha's statue is before the courthouse, folks. Arms outstretched to our people. His words at its base…

(He moves off slowly, looking back at DARROW, NANILOA.)

I'll be back when trial begins –

(He exits.)

NANILOA. *(to DARROW)* "Ua mau ke ea o ka aina I ka pono."

(DARROW looks at her.)

"The Life of the Land is perpetuated by righteousness" is what it means. Mr. Darrow? Sir?

DARROW. *(doffing hat)* Yes?

NANILOA. Aloha!

DARROW. Aloha, ma'am.

NANILOA. I am Naniloa Whitefield Chan.

DARROW. Ma'am?

NANILOA. The prosecutor, Mr. Darrow.

(She offers hand; he seems not to see it or hear what she's said.)

DARROW. Yes, madam?

NANILOA. Deputy district attorney, sir. For the people of the territory, sir.

DARROW. Prosecutor?

NANILOA. Against your clients, sir.

DARROW. *(He shakes her hand, barely looking at her.)* Madam.

NANILOA. I am so honored to meet you, Mr. Darrow, A privilege to serve on the same case –

DARROW. *(baffled by conversation somehow)* Of course – of course –

NANILOA. You are such an idol for me, sir – all your pioneer work – for the colored, the poor, the underprivileged!

DARROW. Prosecutor?

NANILOA. *(She smiles, bows hear slightly in Asian manner.)* Miss Naniloa Whitefield Chan.

DARROW. Chan?

NANILOA. My father was an importer from Shanghai – and "Naniloa"? For my maternal grandmother – a Hawaiian chiefess. An ali'i – royal advisor – to our Queen.

DARROW. Chiefess?

NANILOA. Naniloa *Whitefield* Chan. That's for my maternal grandfather – Jonas Whitefield. Missionary from Massachusetts. Died serving the lepers of Molokai. I am called simply "Naniloa."

DARROW. You're the Prosecutor?

NANILOA. *(smiling, bowing head slightly again, embarrassed but proud)* "Young Portia of Honolulu" they nicknamed me when I won a case for natives' water rights – against plantation owners draining it for themselves! I began in Civil Law, you see. Second woman to ever practice criminal law here now, sir. I will do anything – devote my life, Mr Darrow to helping the underdogs, the suffering people of this earth. As you do.

DARROW. Well – noble ambition – to be sure –

NANILOA. *(still embarrassed but proud)* Educated at Stanford, sir – Law Review.

DARROW. You don't say –

(Sound of gavel is heard.)

NANILOA. *(smiling still, slight bowed head, offering hand:)* A pleasure to meet you, Mr. Darrow.

*(They shake hands as **NANILOA** looks around.)*

But such a "carnival atmosphere" sir, you have brought with you to Honolulu – strange – for a murdered *Hawaiian's* trial?

(He looks at her.)

Aloha…Mr. Darrow – sir –

*(Smiles, bowing head, exits as gavel sounds. **DARROW** exits. Spot on **TOMMY LOU** at desk typing, Morse code beeps. He speaks into mic:)*

REPORTER. WHLU, Tommy Lou at the end of day one of jury selection. And – We have *three* jurors, folks! THREE! Everyone in court then hurrying out – to fresh air.

*(As he speaks, **DARROW** enters new area: hotel bar, sits at table, takes flask from pocket pours it into glass, belts it. Lights cigarette.)*

And – the beach and cold refreshments – I'll be back in court with you tomorrow, folks. Tommy Lou from WHLU signing off…

*(Morse Code beeps. He exits as **DARROW** belts another shot, sits silent, isolated, mood dark. **RUBY** enters, looking for him. Sees him, stops, watching. Then:)*

RUBY. Dee? Dee?

DARROW. Huh? What?

RUBY. It's late. We're missing one of those parties – Mrs. Montegu's friends.

(silence)

I couldn't figure out where you went – so I sent regrets.

(She looks around dark bar.)

Come on out of the bar? Please? You can relax upstairs in our room –

DARROW. Relax? I don't know who the hell I just chose for jurors! Must've spoken six different mother tongues. I don't' know if they understand English at all! And their accents? So thick I couldn't out make if they were saying "yes" or "no"! And oh my God, the odd faces!

(He begins seeing jurors before him:)

Japanese, Portuguese – which they tell me's not exactly Caucasian white – but working class white – whatever the hell that's supposed to mean. Or look like! Then Hawaiians, Chinese, Polynesian, Japanese, Siamese. Then the "mixed bloods." They're the worst! Can't tell who's side their on or what they believe. And then? Their crazy, peculiar behavior!

RUBY. What're you talking about?

DARROW. Half of 'em kept smiling—bowing to me – for no damn reason! Whatever I asked –

(He half rises, imitating this;)

A smile and a little bow!

RUBY. *(chuckling)* Well, it really is the "inscrutable East" then, huh?

DARROW. Stop it! You know I hate stereotyping!

RUBY. Exactly what *you're* doing, Mr. Darrow, sir! Even imitating them? Really, Dee, can't you just keep you sense of humor about it all?

DARROW. I don't find it funny. That all right with you?

(beat)

RUBY. How'd the prosecutor choose his jurors?

DARROW. First off? He's a she!

RUBY. What?

DARROW. As we say in Chicago: "A Lady Law"! And distinguished – and young and beautiful to boot!

RUBY. Really?

DARROW. Worse: she's one of them.

RUBY. Who?

DARROW. "Mixed bloods." Like I told you – the worst of the worst to figure out. She's Hawaiian, Chinese, white. "Hapas" they call em. Looks like 'em. Thinks like 'em. *Is* one of 'em. Knew exactly what how to pick jurors too. And I couldn't read how she was doin' it dime one! Scares me to death!

RUBY. *(laughing a little)* Scared of a young lady Prosecutor? You're just tired and hot – first day – and too much to drink.

(She puts coins on table, helps him up, they start to hotel room.)

DARROW. Worst of it is, I don't know where their prejudices are because I don't know where their loyalties are. You get me?

RUBY. Not exactly

DARROW. I get the jurors through their feelings, right? Biases – prejudices – passions…and I tap into that by knowing their *loyalties*! But are Hawaiian's loyal only to Hawaii? Or us? Chinese only to China? Japanese to Japan? And who're the damned mixed bloods loyal to? Quarter-white, quarter-Chinese—half-Hawaiian?

RUBY. You'll figure it out –

(They enter their hotel room.)

Oh, look what I bought!

*(**RUBY** immediately sliding into a flowery kimono. Twirling in it, then embracing him.)*

Like it?

DARROW. Sure. Sure –

RUBY. Yours is over there.

(She indicates another kimono. No response, he seems preoccupied.)

I ordered room service for dinner, Dee – for us!

*(**DARROW** nods, mind somewhere else.)*

Still worried about that Lady Law and the jurors, huh?

DARROW. Yup!

RUBY. *(helping him out of tie, jacket)* Was just thinking Dee – our local firm's Oriental law clerk – the one who went scouting the neighborhoods for us – he say anything helpful to you?

DARROW. Said in court down here – jurors are gonna *separate* their own *feelings* from their *logical reasoning*, They'll vote on what they decide are the logical reasons for what happened.

RUBY. But that's interesting, Dee.

DARROW. Only I don't understand their feelings – let alone how they reason. So how the hell am I supposed to know how they separate 'em? Jesus Christ!

(**RUBY** *pours them some lemonade, sits down.* **DARROW** *disdains lemonade, pours drink from sideboard. Downs it.*)

RUBY. No more, Dee. You need to think now. Please?

(He puts down glass.)

Occurs to me though – wouldn't be too hard to get to that jury about a mentally troubled man who – in the moment – *can't* separate his logical mind from his feelings – and goes out of control – irrational with those feelings…so he can't think straight.

DARROW. *(contemplating idea)* I don't think –

RUBY. *(interrupting)* What else did this law clerk say – about the natives?

DARROW. Not much – nobody's hostile to our case or me though…and everyone's sorry for the family. Feel they got a bad deal first trial. They've got special sympathy for Theodie.

RUBY. Anything else?

DARROW. Kalani was a professional prize fighter in Honolulu. But born on another island. Here only a couple years. Known as a hothead newcomer that settled everything with his fists…not really accepted – an outcast – whole gang's transient – from different islands – drifters – only together a couple months before Theodie's assault.

(beat)

RUBY. You stop at the DA?

DARROW. Lunchtime.

RUBY. And?

DARROW. He corroborated everything about the first case – whats, whens, whys…

(beat)

RUBY. Dee? All this is tremendously in our favor!

(A silence. Then:)

Know what? David *should* know right away how the jurors are gonna think through things logically so he can give the medical testimony in a way that persuades them to go along.

DARROW. How's he gonna do that?

RUBY. No attempts at sympathy for Johnny's condition – only scientific – logical explanations of his mental state that made him behave like he did –

DARROW. You're right. No reason he can't do that, for God sake! He's a scientific man.

*(Lights up. **STEIN**, in Chicago office, as **DARROW** starts talking on phone, **STEIN** answers:)*

*(talking to **DARROW**)*

David?

DAVID. What's going on?

DARROW. Need to tailor your approach on your testimony, David.

STEIN. What's "tailor" mean?

DARROW. Give the testimony logically – scientifically – 'cause that's how jurors operate here. Keep emotion out it.

STEIN. What's that mean?

DARROW. Emphasize the medical reasons. Physical causes – the science of what happened to Ramsey to make him act like he did – and I'll take it from there!

STEIN. How? You operate on feelings – getting sympathy for your client.

DARROW. Don't have to! I'm gonna try a new way now. New ace up my sleeve. Ruby's idea and I like it.

STEIN. Ruby's? She's making decisions now?

(beat)

DARROW. Ideas, David. I make the decisions.

DAVID. Well – I'll try. Clarence?

DARROW. Yup?

STEIN. Only one boat a week down there from Frisco. I think I could manage to be there by the 12th for you. How's that?

(beat)

DARROW. Week after, David.

STEIN. That's almost start of the trial

DARROW. Time enough for you to examine Ramsey, prep him, then testify.

STEIN. Rather have a few days to settle in – talk with Ramsey – along the lines you want now –

DARROW. Look, David – everyone thinks I'm pleadin code of honor. Wavin' my opening statement, too.

STEIN. Why on earth?

DARROW. I'd have to say just *how* I'm pleadin and *who* I'm pleadin it for. This way nobody knows. The Prosecution starts their case just when you get here. Then? I come in with my temporary insanity plea, calling only the Lieutenant to the stand. Then you testify loaded with science and fact. And there's no time for the Prosecutor to get her psychiatrist to examine the Lieutenant *before* the trial's started. Especially on scientific grounds.

STEIN. But can't she do it at the time?

DARROW. Court here doesn't allow a rebuttal on a witness with *their* psychiatrist *after* trial's underway.

STEIN. Brilliant move!

DARROW. Top of my form, David! Top of my form!

STEIN. Cunning like a fox!

*(Blackout on **STEIN**)*

RUBY. Good idea for you to talk to him about the way to go, huh?

DARROW. You were right. And when you're right, you're right!

(He kisses her. They both laugh.)

RUBY. Here – put this on –

*(She helps **DARROW** into kimono.)*

Oh, don't you just look grand!

(looking at him, then around the room)

Now – soon as room service arrives? We're gonna have dinner, Dee…

(She starts lighting candles.)

By candlelight – by the window – overlooking Waikiki!

End of Act One

ACT TWO

(**REPORTER** *over mic at a desk in courtroom. Mose code beeps:*)

REPORTER. Tom Lou at WHLU now reporting from Honolulu. April 15th. Thursday. Sweltering day predicted, folks – 105 by noon. And Honolulu experiencing an overflow of crowds for the trial! Downtown streets here jammed with spectacle – pageantry we haven't seen since the days our Queen ruled. Speaking to you from the courtroom, folks, where the trial begins shortly.

(**RUBY** *walks in, taking seat in gallery.*)

Mrs. Darrow is here.

(*He looks around, then up.*)

Overhead? Courtroom fans only spinning heat – 100 degrees in here right now – and – our famous mosquitoes?

(*swats his arm, then other arm*)

Everywhere!

(*He chuckles as* **DARROW** *enters, sits.*)

Darrow's in.

(*Gavel sounds.* **NANILOA**, *entering high on level with red lacquered Asian box, containing objects of evidence. Sets this down.*)

Naniloa here..

(**VOICE OF JUSTICE** *is an offstage voice. Should surround theater audience as well as onstage scene. Deep, resonant, authoritative.*)

VOICE OF JUSTICE. ALL RISE! HEAR YE! HEAR YE! THE CITY AND COUNTY COURT OF HONOLULU, THE TERRITORY OF HAWAII VS. MRS. KATHRYN MONTEGU AND LIEUTNENAT JUNIOR GRADE JOHN BIRMINGHAM RAMSEY. COURT IN SESSION NOW! MISS CHAN FOR THE PROECUTION, PLEASE!

REPORTER. Ramsey-Montegu Trials beginning, folks. Let's listen in:

*(Gavel sounds. **NANILOA**, entering high on level with red lacquered Asian box, containing objects of evidence. Sets this down comes toward audience, as if jury.)*

NANILOA. Gentlemen of the jury, The Prosecution intends show the Defendants kidnapped Kim Kalani and – when he wouldn't sign a forced confession – murdered him. Now, we will agree, the District Attorney may well have told the defendants, Kalani wanted to confess – privately – and if he confessed – there might well be only an assault and battery charge for him in a retrial, while the other men would be charged with the rape. And we will agree The District Attorney may well have suggested too that Mrs. Montegu's villa might be just such a private place to sign the confession. And since Kalani reported to probation every day at this courthouse – the courthouse stairs might well be the place to find Kalani leaving each day at around 9 o'clock. But the District Attorney's suggestions, we will show, became only rich fodder for the Defendants! Because on these very courthouse steps, the Defendants first stalked Kalani, then attempted to lure him into the rental car to go to the villa to sign. When he refused, they came back a second day, kidnapped him to the villa, tried to force the signed confession – and when they couldn't get it? Murdered Kalani in cold blood! First evidence of this plan will be witnesses, who on both days in front of this Courthouse, saw the rented black sedan – which hid the Defendants real identities. We will then introduce further proof with testimony from the car rental clerk. And to put into evidence? The receipt from the rental with Lt. Ramsey's signature!

(She pulls receipt from box, displays, puts it back.)

NANILOA. *(cont.)* Further, at Mrs. Montegu's Villa, we intend to prove they murdered Kalani not an hour later with a .32 caliber Colt, which – testimony from the Barley Hardware and Gun Shop proprietor will swear – was exactly the kind of gun Mrs. Montegu had bought there and signed a receipt for.

(She flashes gun and receipt from box, puts them back.)

Next? We will show with Police testimony that as the Defendants raced away to throw Kalani's corpse over a cliff – a Highway Policeman stopped their car for speeding before they could get rid of the corpse. And we intend to prove with the Medical Examiner's testimony – a .32 caliber bullet was found near Kalani's heart, consistent, of course, with bullets used in a .32 caliber Colt! Exactly the type of gun Mrs. Montegu had purchased

VOICE OF JUSTICE. ALL RISE! COURT WILL RECONVENE 9 AM MONDAY APRIL 19TH. COURT NOW IN RECESS!

(Morse code beeps.)

REPORTER. And so this day in Court ends with Naniloa offering intriguing information – displaying the strength, courage and intelligence all of us in Honolulu have come to admire in her.

*(**DARROW** still seated, putting papers in briefcase.)*

Court in a four day recess now, folks – people leaving here – hurrying to swim, boat, relax on their lanais. We'll be back with the trial, Monday, April 19th. Tommy Lou, WHLU, your native Honolulu station now signing off –

*(Morse code beeps. **REPORTER** exits as **RUBY** moves forward to **DARROW**.)*

RUBY. Where did she get all that evidence, Dee? The car? The gun? The witnesses? I went over everything they sent you in Chicago. *None* of that was there.

DARROW. Ruby, don't worry. Come on – let's go get something to eat.

(He gets up, walking, she follows him.)

None of this matters to our case at all. It's all just –

RUBY. *(interrupting:)* You only had three weeks to prepare everything! We depended on these Honolulu lawyers hook, line and sinker. And I don't think they ever gave us one piece of that evidence – the car – rental clerk – gun – gunshop clerk –

(They're out of courtroom by Kamehameha's statue.)

DARROW. There're no discovery laws down here – I don't think they knew what she'd found! She's showboating! Sounds dramatic as hell – doesn't amount to a row of beans! Everyone's told me she's got no significant evidence at all…that the receipt doesn't prove they killed Kalani. Or the gun or the car or witnesses.

RUBY. They're the same people told you these Hawaiians can't be gotten to emotionally, right? Well, you could hear a pin drop the jury was so spellbound by her! Emotion all the way!

DARROW. Doesn't matter the jury got entranced a moment or two. That's not hard evidence. Like blood evidence. Now please? You're making me nervous.

RUBY. I'm not so sure she hasn't got blood evidence, Dee.

DARROW. You remember where that Chinese restaurant was? And the juice stand? I sure could use some cold juice right now –

(He exits, she follows as lights shift to another day. **REPORTER** *enters courtroom. Sits at table, fiddling with mic and wires. Finally, Morse code beeps.)*

REPORTER. I think we're on?

(He looks around, pinging mic. **NANILOA,** *very angry, walks into court, on high platform.* **DARROW** *enters, sits as* **RUBY** *sits in gallery.)*

REPORTER. *(cont.)* We're on! Afternoon, folks. Tommy Lou at WHLU reporting. Sorry about the delay today here, folks – trouble with connections all day – but now it's 2 pm, folks. Afternoon session and nearly three weeks into trial. Most of us believe this may well be the final day for the Prosecution's direct case. Let me catch you up on the important events of the morning: Naniloa has offered an array of witnesses – the medical examiner who testified quote: "Kalani bled very little from the fatal .32 gun wound" unquote. But – her next witness, the official blood lab technician, testified that, quote: "It was determined it *was* Kalani's blood found in the villa." Unquote. Then from police at the murder scene, quote: "Kalani's blood stains were all over Mrs. Montegu's villa – floor, carpets, towels –" unquote –

*(***NANILOA,*** ever more perturbed, throws open box, holds up bloody bath towels, showing them around for all to see.)*

Finally the second police officer testified, quote: "Kalani's blood saturated his trousers and undershorts too which we found at the bottom of a clothes hamper! Their flies ripped open with such violence buttons were broken and fabric torn!"

(She now holds up pants, shorts, from box, displaying them with rage and disgust, coming closer with articles:)

NANILOA. WHAT HAPPENED GENTLEMEN?

(Gavel sound)

The white, Haole Police quickly took possession of Kalani's body when they found it. And took it to be examined. Then to the white, Haole funeral parlor which Hawaiians never use. Then Kalani's mother's brought in and forced to identify her son – from his casket, sealed neck down! Finally? The body's buried *immediately* at sea!

(Gavel sounds again. Defiant, she steps closer, holding out pants, shorts.)

NANILOA. *(cont.)* THIS IS A LYNCHING, GENTLEMEN! CASTRATION "WHITE SOUTHERN STYLE!"

VOICE OF JUSTICE. MISS CHAN TO CHAMBERS! COURT IS IN RECESS!

(Gavel. **NANILOA** *exits.* **RUBY**, *upset, goes to* **DARROW**.*)*

RUBY. RACE! SHE'S PUT IT ALL TOGETHER THAT WAY! NOW SHE'S GONG TO DRAG IT FRONT AND CENTER THROUGH HER WHOLE CASE! Why didn't you object, Dee? You focusing on what's going on?

DARROW. Shh! Reporter's probably listening. She was called to chambers. It'll be handled there. Let's go –

(They exit courtroom, walking toward hotel.)

RUBY. But the jury heard her! You always said that was what was important. And RACE? It's what kept you out of the case first time they asked you here. Only had three weeks to prepare! I went through every scrap – Chester – local lawyers – nothing about that villa. Our law office never privately gave you anything on that villa did they?

DARROW. Doesn't matter, Rube.

RUBY. Could our local lawyers get hold of the report about the bloody clothes at least?

DARROW. That Ramsey went out of his mind is what's important. And that's what I aim to prove. That'll put race at the fringes of the case. And make the blood insignificant too – so will you calm down and c'mon? I need a nap –

(They exit as **REPORTER** *comes to desk and mic.)*

REPORTER. Now? Fourth week of trial with WHLU with Tommy Lou. And court about to start folks. With Mr. Darrow for the Defense!

(gavel)

VOICE OF JUSTICE. MR. DARROW, PLEASE.

DARROW. I hereby enter for U.S. Navy Lieutenant (j.g.) John Birmingham Ramsey, Commander and Engineer S-43 submarine, Pearl Harbor, Territory of Hawaii, U.S. of A. The plea of not guilty! Reason? Temporary insanity.

VOICE OF JUSTICE. THE RECORD WILL SO REFLECT.

(Gavel. **NANILOA** *looks up stunned.)*

NANILOA. I strenuously object. Prosecution was not informed of plea – a customary courtesy here. And – having assumed another plea would be entered, Prosecution has not engaged psychiatrists to examine defendant, so he may be questioned by them in rebuttal. I hereby move a one day postponement to allow Prosecution' psychiatrists to examine Defendant.

VOICE OF JUSTICE. DEFENSE DOES NOT HAVE LEGAL OBLIGATION TO INFORM THE PROSECUTION. MR. DARROW, PLEASE.

DARROW. Gentlemen, Miss Naniloa's accused the Defendants of kidnapping, premeditated murder, and – the worst – most bestial crime known to civilized man: castration! What a crude, lurid crime Miss Naniloa imagines in her wild fantasy was committed. "White Southern Style!"

NANILOA. Objection! Argument! Not evidence!

VOICE OF JUSTICE. SUSTAINED!

DARROW. Well then – "Evidence?" You see there's good reason for that blood evidence folks: "a second wound!"

(He's now very close.)

Undiscovered! Coroner's stated the autopsy wasn't complete: Quote: "exclusive attention only to bullet wound in chest." Unquote. And no body to exhume! If we only had that, we'd knock Miss Naniloa's lurid accusation out of the ring! Because we'd find that second bullet wound. Probably in the abdomen, gentlemen.

Maybe we'd find even more wounds! Profusely bloody, abdominal wounds – ever see one?

(growing very intimate with audience)

DARROW. *(cont.)* An ugly sight, profuse blood! But there it was in that villa. Because shots hit Kalani's chest, then abdomen, too – when he went turncoat on this poor family – demanding money, jewels, using a gentle lady as his shield, then taunting, humiliating the Lieutenant that he'd rape his wife again – which pushed the Lieutenant beyond reason! Until poor Ramsey fired off two shots at the man. Three? Maybe four? Sounds crazy – doesn't it? Well – it was! A crazed mental state that overwhelms reason. A state when men sometimes shoot round after round after round – at their own families – the ground – the ceiling- themselves! In shock! Wild! Dazed! CRAZED! Not accountable! Temporarily insane! – Lieutenant Ramsey's pitiable condition that day, gentlemen. Remembering nothing he did afterwards – when his senses finally returned! I call to the stand now, Lieutenant John Ramsey, please?

*(**NANILOA** is stunned as **RAMSEY** enters, right hand raised, taking stand as he speaks:)*

RAMSEY. I do solemnly swear to tell the truth, the whole truth and nothing but the truth, so help me God.

*(**DARROW** going to him, speaks softly so no one hears:)*

DARROW. You can do it son – strong, brave man – I know you can do this –

(to jury:)

And now, Lieutenant – can you tell us what the District Attorney suggested you do?

RAMSEY. The District Attorney mentioned Kalani reported here everyday, for probation – so we would be able to meet him right outside here and see if he was agreeable. And if so, we could arrange a meeting for a subsequent day.

DARROW. What was your response to these suggestions?

RAMSEY. I drove to the Courthouse with Mrs. Montegu in the rented car.

DARROW. Can you tell us the reason for renting the car?

RAMSEY. Kalani wanted everything kept from his gang. My car's bright yellow – recognized all over Honolulu from the first trial – as I am. So we rented a car and decided Mrs. Montegu'd talk to Kalani since no one knew her.

DARROW. To your knowledge – did she do that?

RAMSEY. She went to the courthouse steps, then I saw Kalani coming, and her speaking to him. She came back and said he'd suggested meeting with us the very next day. Same time. Same place. He was anxious to get "a good deal" – as he called it.

NANILOA. Hearsay.

VOICE OF JUSTICE. SUSTAINED.

DARROW. Can you describe for us what happened the following day, Lieutenant?

RAMSEY. We picked Kalani up next day, got to the villa – but as soon as we were inside – he announced he knew we had "Big Money" and we had to give it to him or he wouldn't sign.

DARROW. So, fair to say he wasn't only after a light sentence – but a pay-off too?

NANILOA. Objection!

VOICE OF JUSTICE. SUSTAINED.

DARROW. What happened next?

RAMSEY. I said we didn't have money in the house. Right then he jerked Mother M.'s pearls off her neck and demanded I give him her "big diamonds" too. I said she had none.

DARROW. And then?

RAMSEY. He pulled a knife and dragged her in front of him. Then started threatening if he didn't get what he wanted – he had men who'd followed us, were parked close by and knew my address. They'd all take us there and gang rape my wife again! In front of us!

NANILOA. Hearsay!

DARROW. The Defendant is entitled to tell the facts of what happened as he observed them.

VOICE OF JUSTICE. OVERRULED!

DARROW. All of what happened terrified you. Fair statement, son?

NANILOA. Leading witness!

VOICE OF JUSTICE. SUSTAINED!

DARROW. How did you feel about what Kalani threatened in the villa, son?

RAMSEY. Terrified! I started not thinking straight. Really panicking. Then he started jerking Mother M. around, screaming to give him her money, diamonds, describing in filthy language what he'd do to her daughter – she seemed about to faint

DARROW. And then?

RAMSEY. *(starts visualizing this:)* I'm going out of control – trying to keep in focus but…I see him, he blurs, see him again…everything blurs. Scared I'll pass out – she'll faint…remembering the desk…gun's…trying to keep steady…get it – inching backwards to drawer knob – trying to steady hand – opening drawer – the gun! I see him – he blurs –

(beat)

DARROW. Now – if I may – going back to December 3, 1931 – a month before the tragedy in the villa – three months after your wife's assault –

RAMSEY. Yes, sir.

DARROW. You were, at that time, trapped in what I'd like to call a "vicious cycle." You'd consulted a private psychiatrist because you found you'd been blanking out with some frequency by that date, and it frightened you. Fair description of what was happening to you, son?

NANILOA. Leading witness!

VOICE OF JUSTICE. SUSTAINED.

DARROW. You consulted a psychiatrist privately because of blackout spells. Correct?

RAMSEY. Yes, sir

DARROW. The psychiatrist analyzed your condition as – let me quote: "stemming from the Lieutenant's deep feelings of humiliation and inadequacy at not getting justice for his assaulted wife." Unquote. As you recall was that an accurate diagnosis of your mental state about a month before the tragedy at the villa?

NANILOA. Leading witness.

VOICE OF JUSTICE. SUSTAINED.

DARROW. Now son, the psychiatrist recommended you ask Navy doctors for transfer on psychiatric grounds. You refused, he gave you sedatives. Your condition worsened – you felt even more engulfed by feelings of humiliation because of his diagnosis, the suggestion of transfer, and the need to take sedatives. True?

NANILOA. Leading witness. In addition witness not qualified to give medical opinion.

VOICE OF JUSTICE. SUSTAINED.

DARROW. On December 9, 1931, Lieutenant, and I'm quoting the psychiatrist's notes: "Lieutenant reported seeing flashes of his wife's beaten face when he blanked out." Unquote. Accurate description as you recall, son?

RAMSEY. Yes sir.

DARROW. Psychiatrist strongly urged you report this to the Navy. But you said no and that you didn't know what to do. Fair statement of your condition and attitude then, son?

RAMSEY. I couldn't find anything to do that I thought would help me. Everything he said made me feel worse.

DARROW. In what way?

RAMSEY. I had to be a man! Get justice for Theodie with a second trial! I couldn't be thought of as a coward who ducked out of everything with a weakling's "medical transfer!" Or "medication"! It was too humiliating, and I can't tolerate humiliation. It affects me very badly, sir. As you described it, sir.

DARROW. And you'd had experiences long before these – of blanking, passing out, time lapses? In humiliating circumstances where you couldn't function and do what was expected of you? Fair statement, son?

RAMSEY. At Annapolis.

DARROW. What happened there?

RAMSEY. I failed to perform maneuvers adequately at sea and was dressed down harshly twice in a row. I started panicking, got dizzy, blanked, then passed out on duty, on ship. I was in infirmary for three months and – and – thought of suicide because I felt so worthless. A chaplain pulled me through –

DARROW. Suicide?

RAMSEY. Yes, sir.

DARROW. Can you describe how you felt last December, son, a month before the tragedy at the villa when you felt you couldn't get justice for Theodie?

NANILOA. Objection! Leading this witness!

VOICE OF JUSTICE. SUSTAINED!

DARROW. Can you describe how you felt last December son?

RAMSEY. Suicidal! Feelings of helplessness and worthlessness overcame me, sir. You know I'm from the Old South – old traditions of chivalry, duty, bravery. I started to feel unworthy of Theodie – my career – everything! A rotten, measly weakling seeing a "head doctor," taking pills to stay steady, for God's sake! I cringed being seen at Pearl. Started eating alone at mess. Then I started getting dizzy and blanking out on sub duty! Risking my men's lives!

(He looks away.)

DARROW. Go on –

RAMSEY. I began to feel I wasn't entitled to anything, sir. Worthless as a man. Like I'd felt at Annapolis – I – I felt overwhelmed – sinking – I thought of drowning myself on duty but that would've implicated the navy – then I got the thought of my gun –

DARROW. When?

RAMSEY. Near Christmas –

DARROW. Less than a month before the meeting at the villa?

RAMSEY. Yes sir. A Sunday – I was waiting for Theodie to get dressed. We had to go to the Admiral's Christmas Party – I was scared I couldn't face it! So – I was trying to relax, build up guts to go – read some kind of cheap newspaper the maid had left behind – but I was feeling so overwhelmed – the season of the year – how I would be at the party – how worthless my whole life had become – then I hit a scandalous article in that paper about Theodie and me – I realized – I couldn't focus – words started blurring – I – I felt dizzy – the room started blanking in and out –

DARROW. Did that phenomena stop?

RAMSEY. I – came to, yes. But I'd lost time –

DARROW. How did you know that?

RAMSEY. I found myself sitting, paper on the floor, fiddling with my gun that I keep stored in another room. Just then Theodie came in –

DARROW. *(patting him on back)* Thank you, son. That'll be all your honor.

(gavel)

VOICE OF JUSTICE. COURT IN SHORT RECESS!

DARROW. *(quietly)* Brave of you, son – good job.

RAMSEY. I couldn't have done it without you – and Dr. Stein's prep!

(RAMSEY, NANILOA *exit.* **DARROW** *sits, going over papers.* **MRS. MONTEGU** *enters.)*

MRS. MONTEGU. Mr. Darrow?

DARROW. Ma'am?

MRS. MONTEGU. You must stop this dreadful plea you've shoved forward.

DARROW. The jury's enthralled! Finally I got 'em! They're buying our case, ma'am and it's in your favor. We're on our way!

MRS. MONTEGU. By making Johnny publicly repeat and twisting out every unspeakable detail in the world of our tragedy? That he became a weak, terrified madman? Popping off a loaded gun? And referring to poor Theodie's humiliation again? And –

DARROW. We're trying to save your lives! Dr. Stein and I and –

MRS. MONTEGU. STEIN? I doubt I will ever forgive your going against my husband, the admiral, and my wishes with this plea. Why wasn't I told? And how could you dare put Theodie up to cajoling me into accepting everything? And secretly take that poor girl's money for DR. STEIN to come here? She's fragile and you very much took advantage of her.

DARROW. She's legal age. Volunteered her own money. And Johnny approved. He's the one on the stand after all.

MRS. MONTEGU. Did it cross your mind Johnny's in a fragile state too?

DARROW. And a fragile state of affairs, madam. You, too.

MRS. MONTEGU. Yes, I am. I'll never be able to show my face in Oyster Bay again.

DARROW. Especially if you're in Oahu prison, ma am!

(ignores her, pours water from pitcher, drinking)

MRS. MONTEGU. I want the plea changed at once!

*(**DARROW** ignores her, continues drinking. Gavel. **RAMSEY** enters, goes to witness box.)*

*(**NANILOA** enters with red box, goes to **RAMSEY**.)*

NANILOA. There's a bathroom directly off the livingroom in The villa. Correct Lieutenant?

RAMSEY. Yes.

NANILOA. Bathroom where Kalani died?

RAMSEY. No.

NANILOA. You remember he didn't?

RAMSEY. I mean Mrs. Montegu told me later.

NANILOA. What?

RAMSEY. He died on the way to the hospital.

NANILOA. When did she say that?

RAMSEY. When we were arrested. I'd come to by then.

NANILOA. Was he in the bathroom?

RAMSEY. No! I mean I don't remember.

NANILOA. So he could have been in the bathroom?

RAMSEY. I don't remember.

NANILOA. Was he shot in the living room?

(She gets the red laquer box.)

RAMSEY. I don't remember –

NANILOA. So it could have been the bathroom?

RAMSEY. I DON'T REMEMBER!

*(**NANILOA** holds up bloody sheet at which **RAMSEY** gazes.)*

NANILOA. You remember this sheet from the villa found wrapped around Kalani's corpse?

RAMSEY. Yes, of course. I saw him wrapped in it after I came to – when we were stopped…also…

NANILOA. What?

RAMSEY. I remember he was shot in the living room.

NANILOA. You remember that?

RAMSEY. I mean I was told that.

NANILOA. Do you remember or were you told anything else that happened in the living room?

RAMSEY. That's where I grabbed the gun.

NANILOA. And you remember shooting Kalani there?

RAMSEY. Yes – I mean no – I mean I remember being in the living room and going for the gun. I've testified to that. After that I blanked. Mother M. said he was shot in the living room.

NANILOA. Why was he in the bathroom?

RAMSEY. I don't remember –

NANILOA. *(holding up bloody towel)* These bathroom towels from the Villa have his blood on them. And traces of his blood were in the shower drain.

(**DARROW** *looks up sharply.*)

Was Kalani in the bathroom shower?

RAMSEY. Yes – I mean Mrs. Montegu told me – we were trying to cleanse his wounds in there then bandage them –

NANILOA. You and your Mother-in-law lifted this seriously wounded heavy weight champ from the living room to the bathroom.

RAMSEY. No!

NANILOA. You didn't lift him.

RAMSEY. NO!

NANILOA. Drag?

RAMSEY. NO!

NANILOA. Roll?

RAMSEY. WALK! He –

NANILOA. Oh? "Walked"? Kalani "walked" to bathroom – and you remember that, right? Gun at his head? Not shot twice in the living room at all, right?

DARROW. Conjecture and Compound!

VOICE OF JUSTICE. SUSTAINED!

NANILOA. Did you tie his hands behind him in the living room when – gun to his head – when he still wouldn't confess?

RAMSEY. NO! I mean I don't remember!

NANILOA. Did he walk to the bathroom gun at his head?

RAMSEY. I don't remember.

NANILOA. But you just said he walked!

RAMSEY. Not with a the gun at his head!

NANILOA. His back?

RAMSEY. I don't remember! And I was told he walked. I don't remember that!

NANILOA. In the bathroom, did you back him into the shower, shoot him in the heart so he slid down, against the back wall in a sitting position?

RAMSEY. I don't remember any of that.

NANILOA. Any of what?

DARROW. Leading witness! Conjecture! Badgering!

VOICE OF JUSTICE. SUSTAINED!

NANILOA. Now you have testified that he walked to the bathroom and was in the shower.

DARROW. He has not!

NANILOA. Did he walk to the bathroom?

RAMSEY. No…Yes – I don't know – I keep telling you everything was told to me by Mrs. Montegu!

NANILOA. After you shot him in the shower – while he was still alive – did she hold the gun on him while you ripped these open?

(She pulls bloody pants, undershorts from box. **DARROW** *jumps up, disturbed.)*

Castrated him? Then turn on the spigot to wash the blood down the drain?

RAMSEY. NO! NO! NO!

NANILOA. Afterwards did you wrap him in the sheet and drag him out?

RAMSEY. NO! THAT WASN'T THE WAY WE –

(Beat. She smiles:)

NANILOA. Oh? What was "the way" then Lieutenant? Why don't you straighten the story out for us?

RAMSEY. I remember nothing. NOTHING!

NANILOA. That will be all Lieutenant. You are excused.

(Gavel. All leave but **DARROW**. **RUBY** *comes in.)*

RUBY. Oh, Lord, Dee – he is remembering – isn't he?

DARROW. She was badgering him – rattling him – so he wasn't perfect. But nothing damaged him very much –

*(***DARROW*** starts pacing.)*

DARROW. *(cont.)* He wasn't thinking straight – so how could he remember details straight? Well – Stein will take care of all this…set everything straight –

RUBY. You sure you're in this all the way, Dee? Committed? Thinking it through straight?

DARROW. God in heaven will you what's got into you? Johnny's the one we're proving wasn't thinking straight, remember?

*(**RUBY** exits as Morse code beeps, as:)*

REPORTER. FLASH! Dr. David Stein, expert psychiatric witness from Leopold Loeb trial is in Honolulu taking the witness stand now – let's listen in:

VOICE OF JUSTICE. HEAR YE! HEAR YE! COURT IN SESSION NOW! MR. DARROW PLEASE!

DARROW. And I call to the stand, Dr. David Stein, please.

*(**STEIN** enters, goes to dock.)*

STEIN. I do solemnly swear to tell the whole truth and nothing but the truth so help me God.

DARROW. Now, Dr. Stein, you are currently director of the Chicago Psychiatric Institute. Am I correct?

STEIN. I am.

DARROW. And this hospital is the chief hospital in the Chicago area for the treatment of the mentally ill. Correct?

STEIN. It is.

DARROW. How long have you been affiliated with Chicago Psychiatric?

STEIN. Nine years –

DARROW. And you graduated from Harvard Medical School in 1918. Correct?

STEIN. Yes sir.

DARROW. Classmate of Karl Menninger's who went on to found the pioneer Menninger Clinic in Topeka Kansas for the mentally ill, correct?

STEIN. Eventually. First, we both went from Harvard – a residency in neuro-psychiatry at Boston Psychopathic.

DARROW. Can you describe what kind of work that hospital did?

STEIN. They were doing ground-breaking work – first place to offer intensive short term treatment for acute conditions. By which I mean short mental lapses. Hospital held the radical view that a mental patient could have short psychotic episodes – which could be chronic but then go into remission allowing the patient to recover and return to society.

DARROW. After this residency what did you do?

STEIN. I affiliated at the State Hospital for the Insane in New York City.

DARROW. What kind of philosophy did this psychiatric facility have, Doctor?

STEIN. It was another a pioneer hospital – breaking from old 19th century ideas that no real treatment, help or rehabilitation were possible for mental conditions. We treated patients in New York to rehabilitate them.

DARROW. Would it be fair to say you were trained to work with patients who could have sporadic mental lapses, but then get better – or recover?

STEIN. Yes.

DARROW. Turning now to this trial, you have examined Lieutenant Ramsey?

STEIN. I have.

DARROW. And reviewed all his medical and psychiatric records?

STEIN. I have, sir.

DARROW. Please give your diagnosis and opinion then – of the mental state Lt. Ramsey was in when that gun went off in Mrs. Montegu's villa?

STEIN. The Lieutenant was suffering from a condition he had suffered from before – as he has testified. He was experiencing something like "a mental bomb" going off in his head.

(**DARROW** *looks out to audience [jury] not sure they've understood or like what they've heard.*)

DARROW. Could you explain the repercussions of this, doctor, for the jury's understanding?

STEIN. Yes. The condition would create a mental phenomena that would cause him to lose his capacity for immediate memory recall.

(**DARROW** *looks again from jury to* **STEIN.**)

DARROW. Further explanation of this concept – in logical, scientific terms?

STEIN. (*Nodding. Trying to explain as* **DARROW** *wants him to:*) Well – to be more scientific – I might explain this as a condition in which one feels a bomb has exploded in one's mind – that is the Lieutenant would have felt a shock – when Kalani betrayed and threatened him. He would have suffered a form of amnesia. Or as it is clinically called: "Shock Amnesia."

(**NANILOA** *rises.*)

NANILOA. Amnesia is not a legal defense!

(**DARROW** *pauses, disarmed, looks quickly at her, back to* **STEIN.**)

DARROW. Any other medical interpretations or definitions you can give us, doctor, for Lt. Ramsey's behavior?

STEIN. One could call it "an uncontrollable impulse."

NANILOA. Not a legal defense.

DARROW. Any other way to describe this condition?

STEIN. (*slightly rattled. Trying hard to do it right:*) A state under which – that is – a state of – "impaired consciousness," I might say – causing defendant to act in an – "automatic or reflexive manner" – and causing patient to frequently display no concern for the usual social conventions. "Somnambulistic ambulatory automatism," I might say.

NANILOA. Not a legal defense.

(**DARROW** *glaring at her, then pacing, disturbed at what's happening, looking around.*)

DARROW. It doesn't matter if it's not a legal defense! He is *explaining!* Now – could this definition be simplified for the layman's understanding?

STEIN. Still simpler terms? Yet medical, scientific terms? Well, – I would say that Ramsey was "temporarily insane" – out of his mind for a brief period of time but then returned to a state of sanity.

(**DARROW** *seeing jury [audience] is not with him.*)

DARROW. But in terms of what happened to him, doctor – what went on medically to the man?

(**STEIN** *trying hard but now struggling as* **DARROW** *looks at jury and keeps studying them during the following:*)

STEIN. He was in a daze – unaware of what was happening – or, again, his condition could be termed "chemical insanity" – yes that's it: "chemical insanity" – which is the long period of tension and emotional excitement Ramsey endured which caused a "change in his body chemistry" as controlled by "the ductless glands" so that Ramsey acted "erratically" when Kalani threatened him. Also –

DARROW. *(interrupting)* That's all!

STEIN. For heaven's sake! I have further testimony prepared. I'd like to provide it for –

DARROW. That's all!

(**NANILOA** *comes forward.*)

NANILOA. Dr. Stein you were paid quite a handsome fee, weren't you sir, to leave your position at a large Chicago hospital for over five weeks, and travel half way round the world?

DARROW. Conjecture!

STEIN. Yes, I was.

NANILOA. Just one further question, doctor. Your testimony is based on only one assumption – that Lieutenant Ramsey believed Kalani was the one who attacked his wife. True, sir?

STEIN. Yes, of course.

NANILOA. So – if Ramsey didn't really believe Kalani attacked his wife, your testimony has *no* value in this case – true?

STEIN. *(angry)* Obviously, madam.

NANILOA. That is all.

(STEIN exits.)

REPORTER. Court is now in recess, folks.

(NANILOA looks triumphantly at DARROW, then exits. DARROW angrily goes to courtyard. RUBY meets him there.)

RUBY. What happened? He was supposed to –

DARROW. He didn't get through to the jury! I had to get him off. Every time he opened his mouth it got worse!

(loudly)

KISS OF DEATH: THE JURY WAS NODDING OFF!

RUBY. *(glancing around)* Shh! You're always telling me people are around. Let's go back to the hotel. Please, Dee?

(She's trying to push him out without being obvious.)

DARROW. *(still loud)* Coughing, sneezing, rattling papers... hand fans going a mile a minute

RUBY. Please! Control yourself!

(continues pushing him out)

DARROW. FI-AS-CO!

RUBY. He should've known how to talk to a jury he's done it so many times. All that gobbledy-gook?

DARROW. I told him to do that. And *you* told me to tell him! You said that was the way to go!

RUBY. You're not thinking straight. The Oriental law clerk said that.

(She takes his arm, they start to walk.)

DARROW. And that Hawaiian princess or whatever the hell she is, rattling him to death. And that question at the end? God, I'm in quicksand, Ruby. He was my rock!

*(**NANILOA** suddenly appears in courtyard on high level [as on steps].)*

NANILOA. The Prosecution wishes to make a statement at this time to the neighborhood press.

*(**REPORTER** appears, stoops to one knee to get his camera flashing on her.)*

We believe in presenting Dr. Stein, the Defense has made a grave error: failed to understand 'simple facts' about us. We trust our own, have very little respect for "WESTERN Medicine" – or "WESTERN Doctors!" Especially this strange new kind: "The Psychiatrist!" Going into people heads and reading their thoughts!

REPORTER. *(calling out:)* So? In a nutshell?

NANILOA. *(laughs at play on words:)* In a "nutshell"? – This Dr. Stein offered diagnoses of the accused:

(She takes out list and rattles these of as the psychobabble they are to her:)

"Shock amnesia." "Uncontrollable impulse state of impaired consciousness." "Somnambulistic ambulatory automatism." "Chemical insanity." "Shock insanity." "Body chemistry change." "Ductless glands." "Automatic reflexive actions." "Moving in a walking daze." "No concern for social conventions"!

*(She looks toward **REPORTER**.)*

In a "nutshell? The diagnosis from the Hawaiian neighborhoods: he is a "witch Doctor"! Evil power! Coming straight from Hell!!

*(She smiles slightly, glances at **DARROW** and **RUBY**, exits. Morse code beeps, as **REPORTER** goes to desk, typing:)*

REPORTER. PSYCHIATRIST STRIKES OUT! NANILOA SCORES HOME RUN!

*(As **RUBY**, **DARROW** walk from area:)*

DARROW. I've got to get to that jury some other way than Stein – somebody else has got to take the stand – somebody who –

(He stops.)

THEODIE!

RUBY. THEODIE?

DARROW. THEODIE!

RUBY. You never wanted her – said she was skittish – nervous like a cat –

DARROW. But she can tell in plain English how he lost his mind – little by little – day by day. NO-body else can do that. She lived with him for God's sake – saw him blanking out – not remembering –

RUBY. You said she was terrified to take the stand and that you'd never make her.

DARROW. They're all a spoiled, pampered lot. I can't cater to her every whim! And when the words "Not Guilty" are heard in a court, Rube? Be surprised how defendants don't give a tinkers' damn how it happened!

(beat)

RUBY. Well – let's hope –

DARROW. Whole town has sympathy for her. She's educated – attractive – and I'll coach her. Besides – she's who I've got!

*(Lights on **THEODIE**, enters, right hand lifted, speaking as she comes.)*

THEODIE. And I do solemnly swear to tell the truth, the whole truth and nothing but the truth. So help me God!

*(She enters witness box, **RUBY** exits, **DARROW** braces himself, goes to **THEODIE**.)*

DARROW. Now, Mrs. Ramsey, your husband grew very thin during the months after the first trial. Not eating at home. Is that true?

THEODIE. He lost twenty pounds in four-months' time.

DARROW. Ever see him so thin before?

THEODIE. At Annapolis, when we were engaged. But after my – my assault – he was much worse.

DARROW. In what way, ma'am?

THEODIE. I'd wake screaming – from a nightmare I'd started having – again and again – was a little girl back at our summer home in Oyster Bay – a hooded horseman – on my father's horse – dragging me...horse stomping me – hooded man trying to rape –

(She stops, clenching her fists.)

DARROW. *(gently:)* Go on, if you can...

THEODIE. I'd wake screaming. Johnny soothing me. Then pacing all night. He couldn't hold down food either. I got so worried about him. We grew very close...loving at that time. He was so sad – so sorry for everything that'd happened to me. Never so caring in his life! Our love bond was perfect...after that night at the Inn...

DARROW. Anything else from your physical or mental condition affect him – to your knowledge?

THEODIE. That we can't have babies – and when they wired my jaw – and I asked him to hold my hand. You could hear me moaning all over the hospital and I was so sorry for him. He was shaking. Later he told me that image of me was what kept flashing before his eyes. – oh, and there ws humiliating gossip around Pearl that he was a coward only fit for desk jobs stateside. And why wasn't he out getting justice for me himself instead of waiting on the law and the retrial?

DARROW. This gossip affect him badly?

NANILOA. Leading witness!

VOICE OF JUSTICE. SUSTAINED!

DARROW. Do you recall how you felt the gossip affected him?

THEODIE. Badly! He wouldn't even leave the house if he could help it! One Sunday we had to go to the Admiral's Christmas party and he'd told me he couldn't. But I said it would look bad not to go. So, he was waiting on me in the livingroom and had been reading some cheap native scandal sheet of the maid's. When I came into the room, he was very upset. It was that article in the newspaper and it was open on the floor and I saw our picture and knew it was the same rotten article I'd read –

(NANILOA looks up quickly, DARROW notices.)

DARROW. Yes?

THEODIE. His .45 was in his lap...he was fussing with it... peculiarly...I took and hid it, sir...and took that paper away, too...

DARROW. Thank you ma'am. That will be all.

(DARROW sits. NANILOA comes forward to THEODIE.)

NANILOA. Now, Mrs. Ramsey, *The Honolulu Sun* is the only weekly Sunday paper there is. So the newspaper you just brought into testimony – and Lieutenant Ramsey brought into testimony – that would've been from our native *Honolulu Sun*, right?

THEODIE. Yes, because the maid always leaves it and finishes it Mondays.

NANILOA. Would the issue be the Sunday, December 19, 1931 issue, if you recall?

THEODIE. Well, it would've had to be, wouldn't it since the Admiral's party was the Sunday before Christmas.

NANILOA. And you had read through that paper that day?

THEODIE. Yes.

NANILOA. And recognized the article about you and your husband that lay at his feet and the article you'd read as one and the same?

THEODIE. Yes.

(Beat. DARROW begins rifling briecase for newspaper but can't find it. NANILOA pulls newspaper from red box.)

NANILOA. December 19, 1931. Honolulu Sun. "Inside the Ramsey Marriage," "Lulu Wonders" column. A picture of you and the Defendant and this: Quote, "Speculation is rising that Theodora Ramsey was planning a divorce months before her assault, in –

THEODIE. *(interrupting:)* WHAT?

DARROW. Rumor! Hearsay! Speculation!

(DARROW enraged.)

NANILOA. Quote: "In point of fact, Theodora Ramsey had booked hotel space from Cook's Travel Honolulu, a month before her assault for a six week stay in Reno, Nevada!"

THEODIE. I have friends in Reno!

DARROW. I beg the Court! Reconsider! Strike entire line of questioning!

VOICE OF JUSTICE. DENIED!

DARROW. Move for MISTRIAL!

VOICE OF JUSTICE. MOTION DENIED! COUNSEL MAY APPEAL! PROSECUTION MAY PROCEED AT THIS TIME!

(DARROW pacing, glaring from NANILOA to audience, thinking.)

NANILOA. There's further substantiation of your impending divorce, Mrs. Ramsey.

(DARROW stops, shaken.)

Profile-questionnaire from The University of Hawaii. And –

DARROW. Violation of confidentiality!

(searching briefcase, documents)

I don't have the questionnaire here –

VOICE OF JUSTICE. Overruled!

NANILOA. Subpoenaed, sir. No discovery laws in Hawaii.

(She takes document from red box.)

THEODIE. I remember nothing about a questionnaire at all!

NANILOA. From the Psychology one course you were enrolled in, July 28, 1931: Question: "Are you married? Yes or no." But you wrote all over the back, quote: "Trapped and want out! Married me for my money and Daddy's advancing his career. They wanted rid of me! Especially DADDY. He was cruel to me in unspeakable ways. Consult you privately?" Unquote.

THEODIE. Some student must've written that as a prank!

NANILOA. Continuing, "Lulu's Column", quote: "It was known the Lieutenant was involved with another sailor's wife, but he danced openly with her at the Inn at an Officer's Dance – publicly humiliating his wife. It was in rage at this that Mrs. Ramsey stormed out."

THEODIE. That's a lie!

(During following, **DARROW** *seems distressed. Focusing now on* **THEODIE,** *he searches intermittently for documents, tapping pen on desk, searching more. Papers fall helter-skelter to floor. He picks them up out of order, crumpled, jams them back in briefcase.)*

NANILOA. Now, you testified you were kidnapped when you left the Ala Waii Inn?

THEODIE. Yes.

NANILOA. Involved in any kidnap plot before?

*(***DARROW** *looking at* **NANILOA,** *is acutely shocked, distressed at line of questioning.)*

THEODIE. Good heavens, no!

*(***NANILOA** *takes document from red box as* **DARROW** *rifles papers, angry, frustrated. Pages scattering. He sinks into chair.)*

NANILOA. Long Island police records show you and your then fiance, Cadet Ramsey, were arrested, taken into custody, jailed, August 24th, 1928, Oyster Bay, Long Island for kidnapping baby, Megan O'Flaherty in pram outside store. You sped to Manhattan...

THEODIE. The baby slept the whole time!

NANILOA. You checked into Delmonico's Hotel, left infant unattended in hotel room, and were arrested dining formally downstairs!

THEODIE. We were kids ourselves!

NANILOA. Defendant Mrs. Katherine Montegu bailed you both out – and made private settlement to the mother.

THEODIE. Mummer knew it was nothing but harmless summer fun!

NANILOA. Having harmless summer fun when you left the Ala Waii Inn, Mrs. Ramsey?

THEODIE. I went for a walk.

NANILOA. On foot?

THEODIE. ON FOOT!

NANILOA. Didn't you drive your car? Park it down by the Beach – then walk across to the Waikiki Dance Pavilion, Mrs. Ramsey?

THEODIE. NO!

NANILOA. To get even with your husband – by flirting with a "Ukulele Music Boy" in the band there?

THEODIE. NO!

NANILOA. Deposition: Suzy Manuu, hat-check girl, Ala Waii Inn. September 19, 19331. Suppressed from rape trial.

(**DARROW** *rises, somewhat out of control.*)

DARROW. ARE WE TRYING THE RAPE CASE AGAIN?!

VOICE OF JUSTICE. OVERRULED!

(**DARROW** *leans heavily on table now, to keep his bearings.*)

NANILOA. Quote: "Midnight and the Haole woman come to my Hat Check: "Give me my scarf!" she say – and she plenty hu hu! So? She leave, and drive her yellow car to John Ena Road. I ending job – so I walking John Ena too. Bimbye – here come Lieutenant husband quick-march-walking-run – and he plenty hu hu too. And li'di and li'dat – did I see him wife? And I don't answer. Then I go to Pavilion. Bimbye – I see her yellow car by beach – but see she laughing at Pavilion! Throw off her scarf, shoes! Swing her hips and barefoot and hula plenty fast with this lolo buggah: "Manuello, Ukulele Music Boy." Then husband coming for her. She grab shoes, jacket, run in her car driver seat. Husband jump in beside. Down Ala Moana Road they go. WHEE!" Unquote. Now, Mrs. Ramsey – isn't this what really happened that night?

THEODIE. None of it – except I got my fringed scarf from that Hatcheck.

NANILOA. Continuing "LuLu": Quote: "Wasn't Mrs. Ramsey driving and drunk – and weren't they in a screaming fight over the Lieutenant's affair and her flirtation – and didn't he punch her then sock her so hard, she hit against the car door which flew open – throwing her to the ground – while he took the wheel and raced away?" Unquote. This was the article that affected the Lieutenant mentally that morning, right?

THEODIE. *(near breaking)* MY HUSBAND WOULDN'T HAVE BEEN AFFECTED BY ANY OF THAT GARBAGE AT ALL BECAUSE IT IS ALL SO FAR FROM THE TRUTH AS TO BE COMICAL – IF OUR FAMILYS' GOOD NAMES – AND LIVES WEREN'T AT STAKE HERE!

NANILOA. Kahawaii Hospital Records. Suppressed from rape trial. Subpoenaed and released this morning –

*(She looks at **DARROW** who can't look back.)*

First, the Emergency Room: quote: "Patient Theodora Ramsey, admitted. Jaw fractures, bleeding, contusions confirm physical attack. But negative for sexual attack. Second Hospital Report – six weeks later: Gynecology Ward. Patient Theodora Ramsey: Negative for pregnancy."

THEODIE. Those report's have mixed me up with someone else.

DARROW. Objection! Violation of patient-doctor confidentiality

VOICE OF JUSTICE. Overruled!

NANILOA. Didn't both you and your husband lie?

THEODIE. No!

NANILOA. Make a plot to blame *Kalani* for your husband's beating *you*? Even add a ficticious gang rape and pregnancy onto the event so everyone would be thrown farther off? Never suspecting your wild flirtation with a strange Hawaiian at a public dance pavilion?

THEODIE. I SAID NO!!

NANILOA. Your pact was thrilling, wasn't it? To prove you both could drown your wild behavior and his savagery to you in our clear blue seas? Get away with murder? Then walk off scot free to your next escapade!

(**THEODIE** *takes a step to move out of dock.*)

THEODIE. Johnny did nothing to me but love and protect me!

NANILOA. And Kalani was an easy target, wasn't he? Because – by sheer luck he and the others left that very Pavilion – around the very same time you walked over there to flirt around!

THEODIE. I was gang raped! And beaten! And impregnated by Kalani and his gang! And there is a wealth of real proof for that! Let me see those stupid documents, will you please?

(**NANILOA** *hands her the papers.*)

Totally incompetent! Misspelled! Pidgin English! What is it you're insinuating with these anyway? Johnny and I aren't in love? That we harm innocent babies? And plot evil together? That it's your third rate college and hospital – and trashy scandal sheets that tell the truth?

(*She is clutching papers, shaking them in fist, starts moving out of dock. To* **NANILOA**:)

I'M AN AMERICAN WOMAN! AND THE PROBLEM HERE IS WE HAVE GOTTEN NO JUSTICE IN THIS GOD-FORSAKEN JUNGLE OF YOURS! THIS KANGAROO COURT! NOT THE RAPE TRIAL AND NOT NOW! I DON'T HAVE TO ANSWER TO YOU!!

(shaking papers, then crumpling and tearing papers)

THEODIE. *(cont.)* Or about these rotten sheets of garbage!

(now indicating audience as if jury before her)

Or to your slant-eyed trash jury!

(Gavel)

VOICE OF JUSTICE. WITNESS TO THE DOCK! ORDER IN THE COURT!

THEODIE. ALL YOU'VE DONE IS HEAP YOUR OWN LEPROUS YELLOW FILTH ON US!

(DARROW *has risen, going toward her, but she moves farther from dock, toward jury.)*

DARROW. Mrs. Ramsey, please – Mrs. Ramsey –

(RAMSEY *and* **MRS. MONTEGU** *enter from anteroom,* **MRS. MONTEGU** *frozen to the spot,* **RAMSEY** *coming forward toward* **THEODIE**. *Gavel sounding. Following overlaps as courtroom slides out of control. Gavel continuing to sound.)*

VOICE OF JUSTICE.

ORDER IN THE COURT! WITNESS TO THE DOCK! ORDER IN THE COURT!

DARROW.

THEODIE! CONTROL YOURSELF! STOP IT! STOP IT!

RAMSEY.

FOR GOD's SAKE! WHAT ARE YOU DOING? FOR GOD's SAKES!!!

NANILOA.

I demand witness be held in contempt of court at this time!

(Gavel sounding)

VOICE OF JUSTICE.

ORDER IN THE COURT OR THE COURT WILL BE CLEARED.

(Gavel continuing. **THEODIE** *starts tearing documents to shreds.)*

THEODIE.
THERE! AND THERE! AND THERE!

(Papers scattering, shredded, to the floor)

VOICE OF JUSTICE.
CLEAR THE COURT! DEFENDANTS REMANDED TO PEARL HARBOR! COUNSEL REPORT TO CHAMBERS!

*(***THEODIE*** continues to shred papers, into smaller and smaller bits. She's hysterical.)*

THEODIE.
AND THERE ! AND THERE!

*(***NANILOA*** exits. ***RAMSEY*** moves to ***THEODIE****, slaps her face, shaking, shoving her to floor:)*

RAMSEY. BITCH! WRECKING US! SPOILED STUPID BITCH!

*(***DARROW*** goes to ***RAMSEY*** restraining him.)*

DARROW. Get hold of yourself!

*(***RAMSEY*** stops. ***DARROW*** helps ***THEODIE*** to her feet. She runs out. A long silence. Then ***MRS. MONTEGU*** moves forward:)*

MRS. MONTEGU. Theodie should never have been dragged up there to start with, Mr. Darrow.

DARROW. She was the best person I had to corroborate Johnny's instability – which she did. And to gain him some measure of sympathy - which she did not.

MRS. MONTEGU. I doubt she's gained any of us sympathy, Mr. Darrow. Tearing up evidence!

DARROW. No one told her to tear up evidence.

MRS. MONTEGU. Well, if you'd've been clever enough to block those lying scandal sheets, and mixed up hospital reports, she wouldn't have had to tear them up, would she?

DARROW. I beg your pardon?

MRS. MONTEGU. We should never have got you down here to start with. Colonel kept on saying what a risk you were. That we should just keep on doing what we'd done with the first trial: masterminded everything from the sidelines. With Chester. But then we had the District Attorney's help...so I was afraid.

DARROW. District Attorney's help?

MRS. MONTEGU. We made a wonderful arrangement with him in the first trial, Mr. Darrow. Almost all that evidence that came in now was suppressed then: filthy Oriental scandal sheets – sneaky, duplicitous Oriental witness – that Suzy What's-her-name – those third rate lab reports. The District Attorney got it all declared "tainted" – "lost" – "inadmissible" –

DARROW. WHAT ARE YOU TELLING ME?

MRS. MONTEGU. Then he confided we'd never get a conviction in a retrial either. Another racial split would kill it – and not enough hard evidence. We'd need something new, strong to win – like a confession!

(**DARROW** *turns away.*)

Someone came right up right then with the idea that all the District Attorney had to say was Kalani'd sent word he wanted to plea bargain and sign a confession.

DARROW. I talked to the District Attorney. He said a native came to him – privately – told him Kalani wanted to confess secretly if –

MRS. MONTEGU. (*interrupting:*) How trusting of "words" you still are, Mr. Darrow! Even when I've told you, haven't I that "words here are so very cheaply bought and sold!"

(*Beat.* **DARROW** *trying to hold of this:*)

DARROW. You set a trap for me down here?

MRS. MONTEGU. Of course this trial, District Attorney's hands were tied: up for re-election – forced to use that willful half-breed girl as Prosecutor to get himself the yellow vote. And wouldn't one just know she'd sneak her way around the yellow police until she turned up that blood evidence and everything else?

(beat)

DARROW. Have you got any idea what you've done to me?

(He staggers, trying to grasp it.)

Who the hell do you think you are that you can use me? Manipulate me? Get me cornered like this down here at the edge of the world? My reputation on the line! I'll be ruined – Made a fool of by you! WHO THE GOD DAMN HELL GAVE YOU THE RIGHT TO DO THAT?

(She regards him coolly. Whistle blows.)

MRS. MONTEGU. My one regret about any of this, Mr. Darrow? We didn't do what Colonel wanted: string that whole pack of yellow dogs up on trees at the very start!

(She exits. A silence. Then:)

RAMSEY. Don't – don't listen to Mother – she means nothing – knows nothing really.

*(**DARROW** regards him.)*

DARROW. She means everything! Knows everything! A liar! Dangerous bigot! Vicious KILLER!

RAMSEY. But Mother's not me!

DARROW. No! You're the ring leader! Mastermind of the rape trial – with Chester, The Colonel, your mother-in-law and the District Attorney's help! And now – with this trial you're stomping on me, my name, my life's work! GOD DAMN YOU TO HELL!

RAMSEY. I did nothing! Unstable, volatile – but innocent!

*(**DARROW** keeps looking at him.)*

DARROW. You are the worst, the most dangerous criminal KILLER of all! You're capable of "impulse insanity violence" all right – but when it's directed at your wife. RIGHT? Or Kalani? Killed by you in pre-meditated cold blood at that villa because he wouldn't sign!

(**RAMSEY** *turns away.*)

DARROW. *(cont.)* You've abused your power! Influence! Entitlements! The honor of the uniform you've got on. And me! I QUIT!

(**RAMSEY** *whirls around to him.* **DARROW** *starts packing up briefcase.*)

Your "bought-off" Honolulu lawyers can close with "the Code of Honor"! And if that doesn't work, dollars to donuts, the Colonel can call President Hoover and get you all "clemency with leniency and mercy"!

(whistle blows)

They're whistling for you now, Lieutenant, aren't they? To take you to your jailboat?

(**RAMSEY** *runs out one way,* **DARROW** *looking after him. Then a beat or two, and he goes back to packing briefcase. Morse code beeps. Lights up:* **REPORTER** *on mic:*)

REPORTER. And now folks, after fifty hours of sequestration, the jury has taken their seats. The vercit is in! Judge on the bench!

(Gavel sounds)

VOICE OF JUSTICE. GUILTY! MANSLAUGHTER! IN THE FIRST DEGREE! SENTENCE: TWENTY YEARS. HARD LABOR. IN OAHU PRISON. WITH NO PAROLE.

(*Gavel sounds.* **NANILOA**, *triumphant, enters, looking over audience's head, as if speaking to justice.*)

NANILOA. I request prisoners be remanded to Oahu Prison at once!

VOICE OF JUSTICE. REQUEST NONAPPLICABLE!

NANILOA. What?

VOICE OF JUSTICE. IN CONSIDERATION OF PETITIONS FROM THE GOVERNOR, CONGRESSMEN, AND THE REPRESENTATIVE TO CONGRESS FROM THE TERRITORY OF HAWAII, ALL BEGGING

MERCY AND LENIENCY – CLEMENCY HAS BEEN GRANTED! SENTENCE COMMUTED TO ONE HOUR! SERVED IN GOVERNOR'S OFFICE: IOLANI PALACE! PRISONERS REPORT TO PALACE IN CUSTODY OF HIGH SHERIFF AT ONCE!

NANILOA. *(Bewildered, not comprehending, looking out, speaking to the* **VOICE OF JUSTICE,** *over the audience:)* WHAT'S HAPPENED HERE?

VOICE OF JUSTICE. CLEMENCY! ONE HOUR IN IOLANI PALACE! CLEMENCY!

NANILOA. Lynch law's legal? The verdict's a farce? There's no righteousness!

VOICE OF JUSTICE. COURT ADJOURNED! HEAR YE!

NANILOA. "Ua mau ke ea o ka aina i ka pono!" The people have been betrayed! And the life of our land!

(Gavel. **NANILOA** *leaves as* **DARROW** *stands stunned.* **RUBY** *hurries in.)*

RUBY. Oh Dee!

DARROW. The last straw, huh? One hour in Iolani Palace? Probably with cocktails! Everything I stand for, everything I wanted ripped to shreds – like she ripped the evidence! You understand I came down here with an important cause! You're with me on that, right, Rube?

(Beat. He starts stuffing briefcase, one way then another, papers falling to floor.)

RUBY. Right with you, Dee. I'm right here.

(Picks up papers handing them to him. A beat.)

But listen – even if you didn't establish your plea – somewhere else – someone else will.

(He snaps briefcase shut. She links her arm in his, they start to walk.)

You opened the door a little more…raised the possibility there could legitimately be such a plea…

DARROW. But I wanted to *establish* it! Secure the Old Man's Legacy down the years –

(They stop. Silence. She looks at him, as he contemplates what he's said. Then:)

DARROW. *(cont.)* God, maybe I wanted it *too much*, huh, Rube? Put blinders round my eyes –

(She looks at him.)

RUBY. Maybe. But your legacy's already secured down the years, Dee. Your reputation – your life's work – it's all right there in place, last time I looked.

(She smiles at him.)

Now come on – let's start packing. A boat sails for Frisco tomorrow I think.

(They start walking again.)

Winter or not – be real good to be back home in Chicago, won't it, Dee?…

*(They are gone. Blackout. Then very bright lights flood stage. Other times, places, other feelings. **NANILOA** comes forward to audience:)*

NANILOA. An old Hawaiian story goes: when the white man came, he said to us: "Look up to the heavens! And pray to our God! And it will go well for you!" And so we did. And then we looked down – and our land was gone! And half our people dead – syphilis, gonorrhea, smallpox, cholera, influenza – that the white man brought to our Paradise!

(She comes closer to audience.)

I lobby for our people now – in Washington – for statehood! A tough, uphill battle against American sugar kings, plantation owners, Washington politics, and the Japanese! For the right to control our own water, crops, land! Life! 'Ua mau ke ea o ka aina i ka pono! It is only righteousness that perpetuates The Life of the Land!"

*(She stands proud as **THEODIE** enters area. To audience:)*

THEODIE. I leave Hawaii hours later at Chester's advice. So there'll be no complaining witness for retrial of the

Rape case. The other men go free. January 6, 1934 – Reno, Nevada...I divorce Johnny. Two years to the day Kim Kalani was shot...strange...chilling coincidence –

(She looks down. **MRS. MONTEGU** *enters, contained, holding back all feelings.)*

MRS. MONTEGU. July 4, 1937. Whimsy Cottage, Oyster Bay...Long Island...New York...our beloved Theodie's taken her own life...this gay holiday weekend...cocktail party time on the veranda...a scream rings out...a bedroom window above...in the garden...Colonel finds her...splayed across a flower bed...

*(***RAMSEY*** comes forward to area. To audience:)*

RAMSEY. December 7, 1941. I am on duty – Pearl Harbor – when the Japanese start bombing – our entire Naval fleet –

(Morse code beeps. **REPORTER**, *older, more established. From his desk, on mic:)*

REPORTER. Tom Lou WHLU reporting. Just back from Pearl Harbor. Shock – chaos everywhere. First casualty lists just posted. USS Oklahoma. Among casualties, folks? From the Montegu-Ramsey trial you may remember from long ago? Captain John Birmingham Ramsey. Killed.

(Morse code beeps. Light down on all except spot on **DARROW** *somewhere else. He seems almost like a portrait.)*

DARROW. I speak and will always speak for the underdog. The wretched, the forgotten of this earth – chased by life, hounded like wolves into dark corners – dungeons from which they can't escape. The wretched of every kind – wretched in body, wretched in spirit – wretched in their *minds!* Those who still have some hope, some undying faith remaining in the institutions of this land – to help them!

End of Play

COSTUME DESCRIPTIONS

CLARENCE DARROW: Red galluses(wide suspenders), string tie, white shirt, crumpled grayish linen suit of the era and hat of the era, kimono.

RUBY DARROW: Simple print dress(es) of period, small heels, cloche hat, chenille robe at start, kimono.

MRS. MONTEGU: Upscale silk dress(es) of period, pearls, small heels, purse, hat(probably cloche)

LT. JOHN RAMSEY: Formal naval officer's summer uniform or parts of it throughout(as appropriate to scene): naval hat, tie, trousers, shirt, shoes.

THEODORA RAMSEY: Slightly "flapper" style clothes. Slightly dramatic. Chiffon, summery, "southern belle flirt" air to her clothing. Wears long chiffon green scarf around her neck that trails down.

NANILOA WHITEFIELD CHAN: Dark crepe dress of the period and a Hawaiian lei.

DR. DAVID STEIN: Doctor's white lab coat, vest, glasses/pinc-nez), smokes pipe. Conservative suit beneath.

TOM LOU: Mix of Hawaiian/American/ Asian clothes of the period. Might have Hawaiian shirt beneath American vest of period, Asian type straw hat – etc.

ABOUT THE AUTHOR

SHIRLEY LAURO's latest play, *The Radiant*, about Marie Curie, and commissioned by Sloan Science Foundation, received its first Workshop at The Actors Studio, June, 2009, starring Angelica Torn. Another recent play, *All Through the Night*, enjoyed its New York premiere at Off-Broadway's Marjorie Deane Little Theater, October, 2009. In Chicago's World Premiere the play received a Joseph Jefferson Nomination as "Best New Chicago Play of the Year" and subsequently was presented by Ashby Stages, Berkley, CA., and Traveling Jewish Theater of San Francisco. It is a Samuel French 2010 publication.

Clarence Darrow's Last Trial, recipient of an NEA "Access to Excellence" grant, a Carbonell nomination as "Best New Play in Florida, and The New American History Play Prize (finalist), is a Samuel French, 2010 publication as well – while her multi-generational play, *Speckled Birds*, will complete the trio of Ms. Lauro's 2010 Samuel French publications. *Audition* was produced at The Cherry Lane Theater, in the Festival: Turning Points, November, 2009.

Edited by Ms. Lauro with Alexis Greene, the anthology, *"FRONT LINES: Political Plays by American Women"*, enjoyed publication by New Press, June, 2009 and was chosen as an "Honoree of The Coalition of Professional NY Women in Arts and Media".

A Piece of My Heart, whose New York Premiere was at Manhattan Theatre Club, has enjoyed over 1,800 productions around the world, Recipient of the Barbara Deming Prize, The Kittredge Prize, The Susan Blackburn Prize (finalist), the play recently was named by Vietnam Vets of America, Inc.: "The most enduring play in the nation on Vietnam."

The Contest, received The Foundation for Jewish Culture Award, was directed by Jerry Zaks for Philadelphia's Annenberg Center, and originally premiered off-Broadway at The Ensemble Studio Theatre. In honor of its Applause publication, Phyllis Newman starred in the celebratory presentation of the play in New York. Samuel French published the acting edition in 2000.

Open Admissions, on Broadway, received one Tony Nomination, two Drama Desk nominations, a theatre World Award, a Samuel French Award, was a *New York Times* pick for "Ten Best Plays of the Year", and received the prestigious Dramatists Guild's Hull-Warriner Award. Ms. Lauro subsequently adapted the play for a CBS TV Special starring Jane Alexander and Estelle Parsons. In 2008 the play was honored by publication in *Writing Through Literature*, where it joined works by Walt Whitman, Ionesco, Langston Hughes and Toni Cade Bambera in the book's section, *"The Lesson"*.

Other work includes: *The Coal Diamond* (Heidemann Prize, Humana Festival; *"The Best Short Play Anthology"*; *NOTHING IMMEDIATE* (OOBA Festival Winner); *Railing It Uptown* (Playscripts, Inc., *"Take Ten Anthology"*); *SUN-*

DAY GO TO MEETIN' ("*30 Plays for Three Actors*", Humana Festival); *Pearls on the Moon* (Ensemble Studio Theatre; Stamford Theatre Works with Joanna Merlin, Pauline Flanagan).

Ms. Lauro's novel, *The Edge* (Doubleday [Hardcover]; Dell[Softcover]): U.S.A., Weidenfeld & Nicolson(Hardcover) English Library(Softcover): Britain, was a Literary Guild Choice.)

Major Fellowships: The Guggenheim, 3 NEAs, The New York Foundation for the Arts. Affiliations: a Director of The Dramatists Guild Foundation, Board Member of League of Professional Theatre Women, Council Member of Ensemble Studio Theatre. Other affiliations: PEN, Writer's Guild East, Author's Guild, Playwrights/Directors Unit of The Actors Studio.

**Also by
Shirley Lauro...**

All Through the Night

Speckled Birds

The Contest

I Don't Know Where You're Coming From at All!

Nothing Immediate

Open Admissions

A Piece of My Heart

Please visit our website **samuelfrench.com** for complete descriptions and licensing information.

www.ingramcontent.com/pod-product-compliance
Lightning Source LLC
Chambersburg PA
CBHW070646300426
44111CB00013B/2293